Jordan Proves the Afterlife

Jordan Proves the Afterlife

Investigating Life After Death Through Science, Religion, and Everything in Between

Dr. George Jawahir

Copyright © 2017 Dr. George Jawahir Medicine Corporation

All rights reserved. No part of this publication may be reproduced, stored in a retrieval system or transmitted, in any form or by any means, electronic, mechanical, recording or otherwise (except brief passages for purposes of review) without the prior permission of the author or a licence from The Canadian Copyright Licensing Agency (Access Copyright). For an Access Copyright licence, visit www.accesscopyright.ca or call toll free to 1-800-893-5777.

Issued in print and electronic formats.
ISBN 978-1-77136-619-9 (paperback).-- 978-1-77136-620-5 (EPUB).-- ISBN 978-1-77136-621-2 (Kindle)

Cover design: Jessica Albert
Cover image credit: iStock
The image on the back cover is a photograph of Jordan Jawahir.

This is an original print edition of *Jordan Proves the Afterlife*.

for Jordan

and all those whose lives he touched

Preface

"Life is difficult," the Buddha said. To figure out this gem of information, he had to sit under a tree for weeks. I did not sit under a tree, but I have had my own enlightenment about life: It sucks, and just when you don't think it can get any worse, real tragedy strikes.

Tragedy struck for me, and that's why I am writing this book. Life was depressing, I was in a rut: although I was successful in my work as a family doctor and working fifteen hours a day, everything else was out of control and falling apart. Then on July 15, 2015, my twenty-two-year-old son, Jordan, developed severe abdominal pain and was pronounced dead within twenty-four hours.

My world fell apart. I had two children, Jordan (b. 1993) and Alannah (b. 1994). Their mom, Kimberley, died in 2006 at age forty-two. There are many times that it seemed I could not survive another grief-filled day. At times, it seems so unimaginable and unreal that Jordan is not here.

I had no intention of ever being free of depression again, but Jordan had other plans for me. I had been in graduate school in neuroscience, in medical school, in the Canadian Armed Forces as a medical officer, and in civilian practice, but none of this had done anything for my outlook on life, death, and the whole series of complications, responsibilities, and rules, except to make me a nihilist: you're born, you're dead; game over, thanks for playing.

Jordan started communicating two days after his death, sending a message that was unique to him. It was specific and timely, and I couldn't believe what I had heard. When we verified what he told us, we found exactly what the message from Jordan said we would. The message was relayed to me by Tony Arpa, a former patient of mine who turned out to be a medium. We had a two-minute cellphone call that came out of the blue.

Jordan continued to communicate, mostly through Tony, and in the six weeks after his death, messages and signs were coming through every day. Never having believed in the afterlife, I just couldn't believe that Jordan was communicating with us – I looked for any other possible explanation. I finally realized that the first message he sent could not have come from anyone but Jordan. It took some time for the implications to sink in.

Jordan still communicates through Tony, who calls me from time to time with messages from Jordan. Exactly how Jordan does this is a mystery to me. What is not in doubt is that it is Jordan. I can understand why he sends us messages. In his new life, he still cares deeply about family and friends. He wants us to know that he is still around and that he's doing okay.

Jordan has now communicated with me through several mediums. I branched out to other mediums to cover as many bases as I could. I looked for consistency across a sample of mediums and across repeated encounters with the same mediums. I really needed to be sure that there was an afterlife, that Jordan was there, and that he was happy.

Many people really want to find out the truth about life, death, and a possible afterlife. They want to know if their deceased loved ones will, once again, be reunited with them. My mission became to find information about the afterlife by using every means available to me. I completed research using books and information online, and I gathered personal information from a number of people to help clarify this issue for myself and others. Well-equipped centres are doing strict scientific studies of mediums' ability to communicate with the deceased, with good success. I'm glad to know that efforts are being made to prove to us there really is existence after death and that our loved ones are sending messages to us that only they could have sent to let us know they're okay.

I started with incredible information from a medium, but I quickly realized that the information I received, though truly special, needed to be verified and shared. I had to start with the facts that I had been assured of in no uncertain terms: Jordan died in this world, but he is more alive today than any of us. With this motivation, but still filled with grief, I set out to find sources of information rooted in fact instead of unfounded opinions on both sides of the afterlife issue. I also had to assess them for merit, as people can twist facts.

Jordan's death has devastated me, but knowing that his personality still survives, surrounded by family and friends, and has a job in the afterlife that he loves – helping young kids cross over – helps me to keep going, to at least give him the tribute his life deserves. From what I have learned, the continuation of life after death is not resting in peace; it is far more real and very active in incredible ways.

That is the beacon of hope that inspired me to share this silver lining around a huge cloud with those who need hope in their darkest hours. I can reach the most people with a book, which I have been instructed by the other side to write. Any criticism or ridicule for my beliefs that come my way are nowhere near as important as getting this information out there to reassure anyone having doubts about life after death.

I'm writing this first for Jordan; his memory cannot be forever lost. He was here, he was special and significant, and he loved and was loved. Second, it is for everyone who needs to know how to connect with loved ones who have made the transition from life to afterlife. Finally, it is for everyone, because we all must contemplate the end of life sooner or later.

Death is not the end, and this is not false hope or wishful thinking – that kind of hope does not last long. I needed to do the work to be sure about an afterlife, not just to deal with my lifelong doubts, but for anyone else who needs to know the truth, whatever that turned out to be. The job was taxing, to say the least. There is so much out there once you start looking. There were moments of doubt when I saw, read, or heard "evidence" that anyone who believes in an afterlife is just fooling themselves. But I dug a little deeper and inevitably found that these people are just wrong, that their opinions are unfounded. They simply had not had the experiences that I – and many others – have had.

The weight of all the evidence collected throughout history leads to only one conclusion: the afterlife exists.

Introduction

This book covers a lot of ground, but the main points of discussion are my personal encounters with the afterlife, the evidence supporting the existence of the afterlife, and the arguments that skeptics put forward to try to disprove its existence.

Within these pages, I also hope to honour my son, Jordan. I would like to tell you a bit about his life before we explore his afterlife.

Jordan's birth was one of the happiest days of my life, just as it was when my daughter Alannah was born. Jordan was an active, bright kid. He was always considered by his teachers to be brilliant, but his work habits were poor. With his innate intelligence, he could accomplish anything he tried. However, this became more difficult as he started to develop the family traits of severe depression and anxiety. Alannah was suffering too. I did not cope well with their problems on my own and kept taking them to therapists. They were not overly receptive to that, and they compensated by always being surrounded by lots of friends. They both seemed carefree and happy on the outside.

Jordan developed another quality that made him much admired: he was a natural leader. People gravitated toward him. Jordan always showed a loving and caring side and helped me when I was low. We had depression in common, and we talked about it.

Jordan was always a great singer. I added videos to YouTube of him at ten years old singing "Blowing in the Wind." I also added some videos of Jordan improvising with his friend Adam on guitar, recorded a few years before he died. His voice had changed, but it was still the best around. He fronted a good band as lead singer, and they were about to start performing in public when he died. He had so much charisma that whenever he sang in a bar, the place was packed. He was admired for his talents and great personality but also for his caring soul.

Around the time he died, Jordan was incredibly frustrated that he had done nothing constructive for seven years, except for singing. Shortly before he died, he got his General Equivalency Diploma (GED) and had a chance to start university as a mature student. He did not like any of the courses offered, and he couldn't decide what to do. He knew he needed to get on with his life, but he didn't have any interests other than music. He was a suffering and conflicted young man when he died.

My son's journey into a new life, and the effort he has put in from the other side, while tremendously sad for me, is also the reason that I am so proud of him. I miss him more than I can express in words, but knowing that he still exists is comforting. It has been said that our time on earth is just a shadow of the glorious life in our real home, the spirit plane, and in this book, I hope that I will be able to give some credibility to that.

The great thing about the afterlife is that a lot is already known about it, and anyone who needs to make contact with a deceased loved one can do so.

After-death communications are reported to come in many forms. They can be picked up by a medium's brain through electrical and electronic mayhem or they can come through a presence, which the living often experience through touch, sounds, and scents. You can find a full list online of ways spirits in the afterlife have been reported to communicate.

I have experienced communications only through mediums. However, I have seen electronics do strange things that are hard or even impossible to explain. I have reason to believe that Jordan has manipulated objects, including writing on an object overnight, and others swear that they have felt his presence strongly. I am sure that many other people have had experiences like these and know that a good afterlife exists but are being told that what they are saying is impossible. I provide examples, both from my experiences and from people everywhere, to show that spirits in the afterlife contact living people. No matter what a few people say, this is as real as it gets.

The information I provide is complete and honest. Jordan has made tremendous efforts to reach out from what I can only describe as the other side to bring us all real hope.

I also discuss common arguments against the afterlife. To counter these arguments, I give more than enough reasons why no one should believe them.

I aim to show not only that mediumship is a viable way to stay connected with the afterlife, but also how some people have a vested interest in trying to disprove the afterlife and how they are mistaken.

Everyone has the right to have an opinion, but if they try to force a false belief on others, that can do damage. I show exactly how their thinking is wrong and closed-minded but is built on deception and an unwillingness to look at the truth when it is right in front of them. I have come to understand why they do this. In this book, I've aimed to do much more than just disprove the theory that death is final, a belief that some people feel everyone should share. For instance, I talk about scientific studies and show how science is able to start telling us that the afterlife does exist. I have learned a lot about mediums first-hand. I want to present what they do differently in-person compared with what they do in their books, in which they often discuss their lives and talk about the many times they have made contact with deceased loved ones to help those of us who miss them.

I now believe that there are a lot of great mediums around, and I try to understand exactly what they do and how they are probably doing it. In chapter two, I do an in-depth interview with one of my own mediums. It is not easy for mediums to have extended contact with the afterlife: each encounter uses up a lot of energy, and they pay that price. Good mediumship can do so much to help people cope with death. It is worth the effort to pursue if you are dealing with a death. Your grief will never go away, but you can have some certainty that you will not be separated forever from those you loved.

I wanted this book to take on a lighter tone after making my case for mediumship and the afterlife, so I look at the many different descriptions of the afterlife, including the totally bizarre ideas some people have. I also look at a lot of information that might be useful in knowing what your loved ones are experiencing. It really sounds like they are in a much better place than we are, but there is a good reason why we are here. Though many of us struggle with life, there is purpose in all of this. I don't restrict myself to any particular religious view of the afterlife. I want this book to be accessible to everyone, regardless of their beliefs.

I want to help people cut through useless information available in books and online and get right to the good information. I also want to know more about the afterlife than what is available currently, and I make a special plea to mediums to spend a little time getting as much information for us as possible.

I have had a series of incredible experiences courtesy of my son after his death. They were not fanciful imaginings to delude myself that Jordan was not completely gone. I am not gullible – I have a background in science, good analytical ability, and I am able to think outside the box for explanations for anything that seems unnatural. But the facts were the facts, and after looking for ways to disprove them and not finding any, I had to admit that I was wrong in my beliefs about death. The only explanation left was that there is a place of living souls outside of our space and time, where our rules of science and logic do not apply.

It is only appropriate that this book starts and ends with Jordan. I end it by summarizing my personal journey, and that of my son after his death.

PART I

My Introduction to the Afterlife and Mediumship

ONE

Jordan's Afterlife Communications

My son, Jordan George Jawahir, was born February 8, 1993, and died July 15, 2015. His death was sudden and unexpected, and my life since then has been devoted to finding out where he is now.

Jordan had been physically healthy all his life, but four months before his death he had been hospitalized and diagnosed with a particularly bad form of pancreatitis. He recovered enough to be managed by some medication and monitoring, but then one night he got severe abdominal pain, and I took him to the hospital. I stayed with him until noon the next day, when I had to go to work.

I gave him a big hug and said, "Jordan, I love you. See you tonight." He said, "I love you too, Dad." That was our last moment together.

I got a call at 8:30 pm from the hospital, and when I got there, I was told Jordan had died from an artery rupturing as a result of pancreatitis. His death was unexpected because most young people do not die from pancreatitis.

My entire world was shattered. I was numb; I couldn't think. Someone led me to Jordan's bedside. I held him and kissed him on the forehead. He was so cold. I kept repeating, "Goodbye, Jordan, I loved you so much, and I will always love you."

His sisters and I went back home and just talked. I kept saying that he went peacefully: "he was free of pain, and he likely thought he was just going to sleep." If Jordan thought he was in trouble, he would have rang the buzzer for a nurse.

After-Death Communications

The second day after Jordan died, strange, unexplainable things started happening.

The writing on the crystal skull

The day after Jordan died, his half-sister Meghan and his friend Mallory offered to tidy up my room. They saw the empty vodka bottle shaped like a skull that Jordan had given me. They thought it was interesting and took a good look at it. The next morning, something seemed different about it. There was writing on the front of it that I had never seen before. It looked like it had been made by a black Magic Marker. It said:

> *Sorry*
> *I Love You*
> *Jordan*

There were two vertical lines with a V on the bottom on each side. The writing was clearly Jordan's, and I would think if Jordan had written it in his lifetime, he would have shown it to me and told me why he did it. I had no idea what the symbols were. I asked Meghan and handed her the skull. She started shaking before she looked at it and said she strongly felt Jordan's presence. She saw the markings and swore that they were not there the day before, and she told me that the symbols were Jordan's way of drawing happy faces. Few people knew that. Mallory confirmed that there was no writing on the skull the day before. I did not examine it myself and did not keep watch over it all night. It's possible they could have both missed seeing the writing the day before, and because I can't attest to all the facts, I have to just say it was very strange.

The lyric book call

Two hours later, everything changed for me. I got a phone call from a former patient of mine who had never called me at home before, Tony Arpa, who said that Jordan had contacted him. Tony had told me during visits to my medical office that he was psychic – a clairvoyant and a medium. I listened politely but never really thought a lot about the paranormal. He said it was urgent, and that there was something I needed to know before I went to the funeral home. He said that Jordan told him that he had a lyric book in his room and wanted the second last entry in it on his death card.

I always used the speaker on my cellphone, and two other people heard the whole brief conversation, which was mostly one way: Tony gave me the information, and I just said I would check. I could not bear to go to his room, as it was just as I had left it when I helped him out of there for the last time. A couple of the girls went down to find a book that was filled with full-length songs, except for the second-last page. It only said:

> *Now I wish you could see*
> *How far I have come*
> *To see me from Heaven*
> *I'll always be your son*
> *You'll be my sunshine*
> *Because those memories together*
> *Keep you in my mind*

No one around Jordan knew Tony or had his phone number, and I had my cellphone on me all the time. In any case, I had never mentioned to anyone that I knew someone who claimed he was a medium, so he could not have gotten that information from anyone that knew Jordan. I did not even know Jordan had a lyric book, so that takes ESP or telepathy out of any consideration. I called Tony back to ask how he got this, if he had seen Jordan or heard a voice aloud, and he said that Jordan just spoke to him inside his brain.

Jordan's guitars

On day four, Tony heard from Jordan again, saying he wanted us to have more proof that he was alive and fine on the other side. Jordan told him that if I checked the room off his bedroom, I would see his guitars arranged in a particular way: two black electric ones on each side with a red bass guitar between and an acoustic one lying off to the side. I rushed downstairs immediately, and it was exactly as he said. Tony still had never been to my house or met anyone in the family until the visitation day. No trickery, just incredibly specific information. Hope was building, and I started really believing.

This was the second piece of incontrovertible evidence that Jordan was communicating after his death. I interviewed Tony in-depth, and he explained that he has had two experiences which could fall under the category of remote viewing, but both involved immediately knowing about murders. He has never had even one instance where he has remotely viewed anything else, especially a closed book in a house he had never been to.

How to decide if afterlife information is real

Tony's messages were the first ones I was given. They were so accurate that they would have proven the afterlife to anyone who was not a long-term disbeliever like I had been. I will go into some detail on how I dissected the first one to look for the truth so that I can honestly say that there is no explanation other than Jordan sending messages from the other side.

I looked for explanations, not fully believing that Tony's messages really had been relayed from Jordan in the afterlife. I didn't want to develop false hope, but there was absolutely nothing in the laws of this universe that could explain what was happening.

I am well informed about most branches of science relevant to something like this, and I have often been told that I am good at thinking outside the box and coming up with explanations that would not occur to others. I wasn't, however, familiar with parapsychology and other sciences dealing with the paranormal, so I did an extensive literature review on the subject., to see if anything other than real mediumship could produce the experiences I've had since Jordan died.

The arguments that skeptics of mediums trot out like a mantra did not apply here. Not one of these criticisms about faking afterlife contact applied here. Here's a list of the most common arguments:

1. Guessing – A medium makes predictions based on knowledge of the deceased, family, friends, acquaintances acquired during the reading, as well as

information in public records. This has happened with some discredited mediums, and every instance has been cited multiple times by skeptics as examples that disprove mediumship.

2. Cold readings – A medium reads body language to come up with facts about the sitter (i.e., the person being read and getting information) and the deceased. It also includes the twenty questions game where the psychic throws a lot of questions and names around until one sticks.

3. Hot readings – In general, a thorough investigation of a person is done before a reading. The medium bugs TV studios and uses detectives to learn all about the sitter, mining obituaries and the internet for information.

4. Super ESP (extrasensory perception) – The medium reads the sitter's mind to find out information about the deceased and then tells the sitter what they think are good messages from the deceased.

5. Secret psychic meetings – A group of psychics get together to exchange information about people they have read.

It was impossible for Tony to *guess* when he told me about Jordan's lyric book. He did not do a cold reading, in which he asked questions or fished for information. He had never been to my house, and he had never met Jordan. Some people claim that mediums get information not from the dead, but that they use Super ESP, and that could not be a factor here because I didn't know about the lyric book, and in any case, doing that goes against their principles of disbelief in the paranormal.

Most mediums don't know who they are going to see until they see them, as it is acceptable to use just a first name in booking.

Psychics getting together and sharing information on people they have read doesn't make a lot of sense: if one psychic has gotten information from the deceased, then the phenomenon is real, and I don't think there are psychic cabals meeting in secret to share information. What are the chances that someone would visit two psychics in that secret group? By far the most ridiculous statement one debunker made claimed that psychics have access to a supercomputer with all the information on everyone living or dead.

I have considered and discounted these explanations in all the readings I've had done. In the readings done in person, I am careful not to give information away with my body language, facial expressions, or tone of voice, and no one has ever played twenty questions with me. The one bad medium I saw told me absolutely nothing of value, so she was neither a skilled medium nor a good trickster.

Electronic malfunctions

Several of these occurred at various times in the first six weeks after Jordan left us.

The night after Jordan died, lights were going on and off at random. I didn't think much of this – I only thought that I needed to get an electrician. Then they stopped after a couple of days.

Jordan's half-sister, Meghan, who was incredibly close to Jordan, tells me that lights still behave strangely wherever she is. I have read accounts of electric lights doing this after someone has died.

Cellphones would briefly cut off calls as soon as Jordan's name was mentioned, then everything would go back to normal.

Meghan and I plugged our laptops in to charge. Both stayed at 82 percent and 18 percent respectively, both chargers' lights were on but for eight hours neither computer lost or gained charge, even though I used mine. We kept checking every hour, and it was getting a bit frustrating, as I thought that I was going to have to buy a new computer. Then after eight hours, both just started recharging normally. Meghan took her laptop to a computer specialist even though it was working normally again. The specialist checked it and said what had happened was impossible, that computers simply cannot be made to do that.

I needed a recording of the kids in concert in 2003 for the TV at the funeral home. The recording was on a VHS tape, so I got a VCR to play it. Static occurred only for the three minutes during Jordan's solo of "Blowing in The Wind." Two tapes did the same thing for nearly an hour. When I had lost patience (and got tired of swearing at the unit), it suddenly played the whole fifteen-minute tape without static. I got a DVD made and everything was fine. The cellphones and VCR issue were strange, but the computer charging issue was impossible. Tony said that Jordan had told him it was easy to mess around with anything electrical, and that he would show us this.

Possible prescience of impending death

One week before his death, Jordan's band was rehearsing a song with the words *your vacant eyes will haunt me*. Jordan insisted in singing it as *my vacant eyes will haunt you*, against strenuous objections from the rest of the band.

A few days before he died, he got dressed up in a suit and tie for no reason and asked a friend to take a picture. This ended up as the picture on his death card.

There are two more things that suggest that Jordan could have manipulated things on this plane after death.

Safety pins

Meghan and I went to the bar where Jordan had sung in (and won) karaoke contests several nights a week after hearing that they had put up his death card on a special board. We wanted to thank them for honouring him. One bartender said that there were fifty of his friends in the bar right after the funeral, and she asked if they had name tags with safety pins because after they left, the floor was littered with pins. No one wore name tags, and who would carry a bagful of safety pins after a funeral to scatter all over the floor? I suppose one prankster could have done that, but what was unbelievable was that for the next three days, when they opened the bar, safety pins were all over the floor, even behind the bar. The only explanation would be that someone broke into the bar nightly to scatter pins, or that she was lying for no reason, but we asked the other bartender, and she confirmed the story.

I later read about Bishop James Pike, who was in England in 1966, when his twenty-two-year-old son shot himself in a hotel room in New York. After that, safety pins showed up multiple places in his apartment, opened to indicate 8:19 or 8:20, the time of the suicide.

Elevators

On Christmas Day I was an inpatient in a hospital for grief, loss, and depression treatment. Every time I approached the elevator, the doors opened before I got to within a few feet, but the elevator was empty. After the sixth time, I said "Jordan, can you keep this up all day?" It happened every time I went near the elevators – twelve times in all. Someone on another floor would have had to push the button for my floor and gotten out each time it happened. There were no sensing devices that would pick up anyone approaching the elevator and no hidden cameras that could be monitored from another floor, and even if someone had access to one, who would sit there watching it all of Christmas Day just to mess with my head? The elevator had never done it before that day, and it never did that during the rest of the time I was there. I really thought I could feel Jordan's presence.

It may well be just my imagination, but it felt like the best Christmas gift I could hope for.

Ongoing signs

Tony always seems to call when I haven't eaten or slept properly for a few days, and I'm in my lowest depression. He always says Jordan told him to tell me not to get down and to get on with living my life.

Tony was sitting in a coffee shop with his partner, Suzanne, talking about psychic things in general when a young woman at the next table approached them. Tony says he heard Jordan clearly say, "I know her, ask her." He asked her if she knew Jordan Jawahir. She said yes, but he had died two years before. When he told her that Jordan had told him to ask, she was stunned. I can't explain that either.

Second death anniversary – the baseball sign

Tony called me on July 15, 2017, to say that Jordan was showing him a baseball full of names on it and images of him as a child rolling it across the carpet. I had forgotten that I had an autographed souvenir Toronto Blue Jays ball from the World Series in 1992. Jordan had played with this as a kid. Not to belabour the point, but this is something I had forgotten. I don't even know where the ball is. No way could Tony have come up with this without getting a message. Jordan would have known that the anniversary of his death was going to be an unbearably sad day for me, and he helped yet again.

For all these incredible signs and messages, I am grateful to my son, but I still miss him more than I can say. Tony isn't the only medium I've seen. I have seen other psychic practitioners to see if communication with Jordan could happen with other psychic mediums.

Other Mediums

I had begun to believe that Jordan was a special and powerful soul with the ability to communicate with us freely when we needed him, and I believe that anyone in my shoes who experienced what I did repeatedly would be equally convinced.

For research purposes, I wanted an even more airtight case. Really, I was looking for as much contact with Jordan as possible, but I also wanted to see how other mediums worked. The first one was a complete disaster. I will tell that story in chapter three, where I discuss bad mediums. I will also be as brief as possible about my visits with the other mediums, as there was so much said at each session. Here are the highlights.

Dora

Dora's website (mediumdora.ca) advertised that she was a transfiguration medium. Those that made contact with her would fashion copies of their faces – and in some cases their entire bodies – from ectoplasm. Obviously, I was intrigued, but I was not going to be taken in again. She charged $150 for a one-hour session, but ended up spending almost four hours with me for no additional fee. She was, in my estimation, honest and sincere about what she did.

The failures in this session were largely my fault. I found out that when I'm asked to do something, to co-operate with a medium, I am unable to just let things happen; I try to force the session to show me what I want to see instead of letting go, clearing my mind, and allowing spirits to do what they need to do. I want them to perform as per my agenda. As a sitter, that sabotages a session. I am much better when people just pass messages on to me, because then I don't have to do things like let go of expectations. It has been a lifelong problem; I'm controlling, and I have frustrated many therapists with my need to control everything (even how they do their jobs).

After a nerve-racking 90-minute drive in a snowstorm, I needed to relax. I asked if she could do a regular reading for a bit. She said after a few minutes that she could see Jordan pointing at his hair and laughing. A start: Jordan always thought it was funny that I cut my own hair.

Then she dropped a bombshell: Jordan had his arm around a pretty, young, dark-haired girl about twenty years old that he insisted was his sister. Dora asked if Jordan's mom, Kim, had had a miscarriage. Close, she'd had a therapeutic abortion about twenty years before. That was an event I have never mentioned to anyone. It was a difficult time, and Kim and I had kept that to ourselves. I was not even thinking of that at the time she brought it up. Now I really want to see my daughter, who I never knew. I hope she is still there when I get there. I must ask Jordan to ask her stick around until I get to the afterlife. However, I don't feel I deserve that honour – another dose of guilt added here.

I later found out miscarriages and infants who die grow up on the other side. I told Tony later that I forgot to ask for a name. He said he was getting Angelina or Angelique – my sister and mother's middle name was Angela.

After a break, we tried the transfiguration.

Surprisingly, my dad, who died at Christmas in 1996 after a stroke that had him comatose for a week, was the first face I saw forming. I wondered why him, since I wanted to see Jordan, but it was still nice to know that he was helping in the session. Then I remembered Jordan coming into my room on that day, saying that a boy wanted him to come out and play. He said it sounded like it was Grandpa. Thirty minutes later, my mom called from Florida to tell me my dad had died thirty minutes before.

I then saw fleeting images of Jordan, alone and with Kim. All the images appeared in front of Dora's face. They were brief and never fully formed. I saw my mom and my grandmother as a young woman. Finally, she said a doctor friend of mine had passed and he wanted to come through. I gave verbal permission to Rick. When I did, his face started to form, unmistakably him, but again it was brief.

Dora noticed that I was thinking too much, trying to will things. She mentioned this to me, and she wanted me to see something, so she asked if I wanted to see an alien. Only then did I see her face morph into an elongated, thin head, with yellowish skin and a ridge on the head. That one lasted, but obviously had no message, likely because I had no strong emotional investment in any aliens. I am fully aware that the alien thing sounds crazy, but I promised to tell everything as it happened. Why aliens appeared, I'm not sure.

I got some useful information from the session. Dora would be a great medium for a sitter who hasn't got a war going on in their own head. If you're interested, you can find her website at mediumdora.ca.

Dora asked me to add to the book a phrase from her website, "Seeing is Believing." I know that I saw a clear transformation in her face at the end. This is even stranger because I saw that same face when the next medium I saw months later had that alien as one of his five spirit guides.

I won't go into the topic of spirit guides that help mediums; most mediums that write books go into this in detail. Are spirit guides proof of the afterlife for humans? I don't know, but many mediums say that their guides were once human. No spirit guide has ever appeared to me, but my lack of any mediumship ability is not the issue here.

I have spoken with Dora several times, after the first draft of this book, and she has mentioned something that may provide more evidence of an afterlife. She has on occasion helped the police with a missing person, but she cannot talk about this in detail.

I reviewed the evidence for this to see if mediums have received information from deceased people that has helped the police solve cold cases. Mediums are not usually involved in cases until a victim's family member has contacted the medium, received information, and persuaded the police to reopen the case. I think murderers have been caught because of the physical evidence found at the guidance of the medium. However, the information online is contradictory on this point: there are claims that psychics and some mediums have helped the police, but others say they were more of a nuisance.

A medium once apparently taught courses for the FBI, but it isn't clear what she was doing there. The website victorzammit.com, in a series of articles on a hypothetical cross-examination of James Randi, cited numerous cases in Florida where mediums or psychics gave police information about where to look for evidence, and he quotes the officers as saying that they would likely not have solved the cases without paranormal help, but I did not find original press reporting on this.

Mark

My friend, Ann, lost a son in his teens. Ann found a medium who helped her talk to her son and reassure her that he was all right. Mark Hamilton had an eight-month wait-list, but I agreed that she could give him my first name and phone number. I was surprised to get a call from him the very next day telling me he wanted to see me the following day. When I got there, he was pacing. His first words were, "Your son Jordan has a very strong spirit. He showed up yesterday and wouldn't leave until I booked you. It was affecting my ability to work with other clients." He knew it was my son, and he knew his name. He wasn't told before. He could have traced the cell number and used Google, but this is a busy man, in no need of more clients, and he seemed extremely sincere and honest.

This was a different type of session. I didn't ask any questions; he just told me things. I listened and asked for clarification. I didn't like what I was hearing. Fake mediums don't tell a client upsetting things. There were some comforting things as well, but overall I was told that my deceased son and my family members who had passed were telling him about a lot of concerns they had.

He showed me pictures of his spirit guides. The fifth one was the exact same alien Dora had shown me.

He said Jordan was flashing him the word *structure*. It was the first thing he said as soon as I sat down. I knew I had provided Jordan with material things, but little structure or discipline. Though his dying was alcohol related , my family situation was not mentioned, still this was not ironclad evidence of contact, since kids who die at Jordan's age usually die from substance abuse or accidents. A few have lifelong illnesses that take their lives, but it's rare.

At the same time, he said that Jordan said I was the best dad he could have and that he loved me, but there was absolutely nothing I could have done about his drinking. I had gotten him into a treatment centre, and he lasted only two days. Jordan said he drank because he liked it. Dora had said Jordan was saying *suicide* to her, but in one session with Mark, a year later, he said that Jordan had realized after reflecting on it in the afterlife, that he had thought he was invincible and did not believe that alcohol could kill him. I had gone in there full of guilt, and while I was told that I was not to blame, I didn't feel any better.

Mark told me that my family members in the afterlife were concerned about my increasing use of alcohol and drugs to cope, and the way I was letting my health deteriorate. To top it off, my mother said she never understood me. I knew that already. She was a teacher – a pillar of the community – and I was doing my best to disgrace the family, and putting my medical career at risk.

Mark was hearing a lot about me and my reputation from the other side. This wasn't information I had given him, and I even tried to deny that I was using alcohol or non-prescribed medications. I didn't volunteer that I had prescription narcotics, and I flat-out lied about the alcohol, saying I might have a small drink on the nights I couldn't sleep. In reality, I was using a lot more. I had spent my whole life denying my alcohol use, and I had become very practised at not changing expression, fidgeting, or showing any distress in my voice about lying. Mark, if he was guessing, would have had to be a better reader of when an alcoholic is lying than people who treat alcoholism because he kept insisting that what I was saying was not what he was being told.

He was also told I had a bad heart and was a heavy smoker. This was true. I have two of three arteries blocked, and the last one is heading that way. Once the truth was out in the open, I resorted to the usual smoker's excuse that it helped stress, which was as bad for your heart as smoking.

Maybe he could smell smoke on me, but Tony also mentioned that the people on the other side, especially my mom, had been telling him these concerns for years. I just blew it off, without even thinking about it, every time. My late mom talking to a psychic about me? Yeah right. Mark also informed me that he was getting the strong message that I needed to keep Jordan's memory alive by *writing a book*, and the other side would not let me die until I had done that. That was the first mention of this by anyone, and I was not thrilled. I don't know how a person can look at another person and conclude that they are capable of writing a book. It's possible that because I was educated, Mark assumed I could write a book. However, family doctors tend not to be big on authorship, so this came out of the blue, and it did not make me the least bit happy. I had done a lot of research, but that was just for my benefit, not to slave away writing a book. After putting it off for over a year, I finally gave in and tried, and slaving away is putting it mildly.

The idea of my writing something that other people would want to read seemed impossible, and as I am finishing it up, there is the new time and energy consuming task of getting it published and putting it into circulation in any meaningful way. But for those talking to Mark, this was apparently non-negotiable. The whole thing seemed unfair to me. I wanted to do anything for Jordan, but this seemed like a bit too much.

My stepdaughter, Meghan, drove me to my second session. I did not tell his office I was bringing her. He had never met her, but before we could even sit down, he asked, "Is your name Meghan?" It could just as easily have been Alannah, a fifty-fifty chance. What followed next has zero chance of being explained. He said, "Your friend Angela, who died of a double drug overdose last year in Montreal, is here and insisting on being heard first. She wants you to tell her mom that she is sorry, and loves her, and is fine in her new life." While the message seems generic, I could not believe what I was hearing. I didn't even know Angela, and I have no idea how he could have known the details of her death, which occurred in another city over a year before. If he knew Meghan was coming, which he didn't, he may have looked up something on the internet, but Meghan had never used her real name there.

As for the message, we can't judge what is important to spirits – not everyone feels the need to give the large amount of specific information Jordan does. It was just a few minutes, but as proof of the afterlife, this message to Meghan was absolutely mind-blowing. It was downright impossible for Mark to know about Angela unless she communicated with him from the spirit world. This is one for which I would like to get an explanation from a denier, or a whole panel of them. I'm certain they can't come up with one. Deniers would just say it never happened, but I was right there, and we were barely in the room when Mark dropped this bombshell.

He told me that I had to come back to Earth again, in a future life, to deal with alcoholism. Why? Am I going to do better next time? And if God experiences the physical plane through us, why does he need to keep experiencing hangovers, with vomiting and shakes? He said that he must come back to work on patience. I would trade the addiction sentence for that any day. This reincarnation belief is common, and again, it was not something I wanted to hear. I really do not want another go at living on Earth.

Mark gave me more validating information of Jordan's ongoing interest by telling me that Jordan now spends his time in an area of our house, to the left of the top of three flights of stairs. I lived in the master bedroom while Jordan lived, but moved to the room in exactly the spot he described due to renovations well after his death. Meghan's dog Shayla, who Jordan had picked out for her, stands in that spot and barks but is quiet anywhere else. These are not things a person can guess or figure out, never having seen my house.

And Mark kept on my case about the book, which I had not even started.

At the most recent visit, he told me Jordan was coming through with a young man his age. Tony had told me the same thing two months earlier. I didn't know who it could be, and I don't know how mediums can know this stuff. When mediums who don't know each other validate each other's statements, the statements approach credible evidence. One medium might guess at something like that, and probably be wrong, but two saying the same odd thing is something else. It's not quite as good as the lyric book, the guitars, or the message from Angela, but it's still pretty good. So, the evidence was building, and highly validating information just kept coming.

Mark accurately told me that not only did I have heart disease but also liver disease and kidney disease. The liver one was easy, but the kidney problem I was just beginning to suspect, diagnosing myself. He said he knew I wanted to "go north." He explained that he meant I wanted to die. But heavy drinking was not going to do it. Drinking was just causing delays in finishing the book, and I am not allowed to die until it is done.

Alfina

Alfina (@alfinapsychicmedium on Facebook) is a medium Tony had known for a long time. He said she was good and that I might get different information from her. He had been completely out of touch with her for many years, so all he could do was give me a name. As a disclaimer, Alfina had been in my office briefly once when she drove Tony there many years before. But I was a blank slate to her when I saw her all those years later, and she certainly knew nothing about the past ten years of my life. She charged a small amount (seventy-five dollars) and spent a lot of time with me. (On that note, Tony doesn't charge me anything – the argument that psychics rip off the public with high fees is invalid here.) Alfina only started charging a small amount as she was deluged by requests for free readings, and the setting of a small fee was to try to stem the flow of these requests. She was hoping to deter the people who just wanted readings because they were curious and focus instead on people who needed to get in touch with a close loved one they had lost.

The first thing she said was "Who is Justin that was with Jordan?" Three mediums in a row told me that Jordan shows up with a friend his age. I did not know anyone by that name that had died.

She accurately said I was writing a book and was getting bogged down and going nowhere with it because I was writing two different books. She suggested that I needed to get "all those books of notes" and separate them, and focus on one topic. This was right after querying who was with Jordan, and the only words I had uttered were polite greetings. I told her that I had no clue who Justin was and said nothing about the two other mediums that had mentioned him, even after she told me. I was trying to just listen and to not speak, only replying to her after she said something unexpected, and confining my response to "I think you're right about that one." To get validation, and be told things of evidential value, I was saying as little as possible, even at the risk of seeming impolite. So now I had three mediums, including Tony, who won't let the book thing go. I was hoping they would drop it and save me a lot of work.

Again, different mediums were validating the others in two separate areas: Jordan's friend and the book. It was all impressive and hard to explain. There really couldn't have been any collusion between mediums, two of whom didn't know of each other, and Tony had not spoken to Alfina in years and didn't even know where she lived.

Alfina said Jordan was with my mom, who was protecting him. I guess they can bilocate – here with a friend, there with my mom. There are reports of living people bilocating in comprehensive books published by Reader's Digest (*Unseen World* in 2008 and *Unsolved Mysteries of the Past* in 1991). It must be a lot easier for a spirit.

Jordan's mom was on the other side of him, so Alfina knew Kim had also passed. I forgot to ask if someone had told her Kim died young, is not something anyone would assume – Kim was younger than me and I'm still here, bad habits and all.

She said Jordan told her I did not have his ashes – right again; Alannah has them because I don't see any value in ashes.

She also said he was concerned about his lyric book, as he wanted some of his songs performed by someone. This was yet another direct hit with no prior knowledge. I had confirmed with her that she hadn't spoken to Tony for years. Unfortunately I don't know where that book is now. As I said before, it was a hectic time. People were grabbing souvenirs of Jordan, and I don't know where some of them are.

Alfina surprised me by saying that Jordan wanted his name in stone – he was not specific, so we may get a stone engraved on a park bench and donate it to the city. The information that a medium supplies does not always have to be about something the sitter knows and can verify. Some information is simply useful but doesn't act as proof of contact. But I can't say she was wrong either. Her track record has been perfect so far.

She said that those on the other side knew I had stopped taking all my heart medications, and I needed to start taking them – you don't argue with a spirit. I don't go around announcing to people that I have heart disease, since people would try to convince me to get that fixed, and hospital admissions, and invasive procedures, are not something I ever want to experience again.

She told me that Jordan knew I was unhappy they had dressed him in a blue sweater vest for the funeral, but he liked it as blue was his favourite colour. I had forgotten I'd complained about that. This again is another example of information that she couldn't possibly have known on her own. I had not thought of that incident in a long time and wasn't thinking about it when I was sitting with her. It's far-fetched to think she could guess about the sweater vest, being such unusual funeral clothing, and then assume I was unhappy about being overruled.

Alfina just kept throwing out what are called dazzle hits in judging mediumship. Tony had told me things that were similarly amazing, but I get these one at a time as Jordan feels I need them. This was a torrent of information coming at me. The other mediums had done some incredible things as well that pointed squarely to contact with another plane, but this was the first session where the medium mentioned things she could not possibly know, and for that matter, in most cases, the other mediums would not have known. Alfina is an exceptionally good medium.

There was one thing she said that I thought was wrong. She said there was a scare about Jordan's health when he was six or seven. I was thinking about serious illness like cancer, and said I didn't think so. When I got home it finally hit me. At that age, Jordan was in Bolton, Ontario, visiting his sisters, and he tried to ride a bike down a playground slide and had a bad crash. His face was split open, and he had to go to an ER an hour away. I took off immediately and bought a pack of cigarettes after two months of not smoking – I needed calming down after the accident. He was in bad shape, but they managed to stitch everything up. Seeing him like that was scary. I called her the next day to let her know that she was right. She had stuck to her guns, and kept repeating this to me.

It would be mind-boggling to me if all these mediums had communicated with each other, for little or no financial gain, over an almost two-year period, just to mislead me about the afterlife. I have always kept looking at all possibilities that this information was not coming from a source, or sources, that had passed on. I do this because I am really sincere when I say that I never want to be wrong about this new belief. I do not want false comfort. I suffer anyway, and I don't think I could possibly feel any more pain from the loss of Jordan, even if I thought he had simply become non-existent.

That's my experience with some good mediums. My experiences over many sessions with them approached clear validation of the afterlife, and because of this I believe Jordan died but exists and is communicating from the afterlife. Everyone else that has died should be no different. It's been over two years since he passed and Jordan continues to give me proof that he is aware of the things that are happening. Most people would be convinced if they got even a quarter of the evidence I received, but I have a greater need for constant and ongoing evidence because I start rationalizing things away, and I am prone to doubt. I believe that extraordinary claims require an extraordinary level of evidence, and the afterlife has always been as extraordinary as it gets for me.

To be honest, I did not want to consider an afterlife – that had always seemed like religious superstition to me, but there it was staring at me in the face. A lifetime of thinking that Mark Twain was right in his response when he was asked what he thought about what after death was like, and he said it was exactly like before you were born, non-existence. I don't know how many times, over the years, I had repeated this to others when they tried to tell me about paranormal beliefs. To be honest, at the time, I felt that I was a realistic intellectual and they were superstitious. Now I feel like an idiot for that.

Today, as I am writing this, Meghan is telling me about a time she was out walking with friends in the woods after dark and was one step away from walking right off a cliff, when she felt some force pull her backwards, saving her life. The friends she was with said it looked as though something threw her backwards. She says she felt Jordan's presence. This is anecdotal evidence, I know. But it is real to the people who have had these experiences, and given many of the things I was told, and have seen, any rational person would have no choice but to know that an afterlife exists and that our loved ones are there.

TWO

Interview with Medium Tony Arpa

Tony Arpa is the most multitalented medium I have ever seen. The fact that he was my patient once has nothing to do with my evaluation of him, as all his messages from the afterlife, which started just two days after Jordan died, have been inexplicable, highly specific, unique, and accurate. A lot of mediums will tell you to wait before trying to connect with them through a medium because the deceased has a lot to go through before they can start communicating. I have been told that only a strong spirit starts immediate communication and does so without being summoned in a reading.

I thought it best to write this as a narrative, based on a question-and-answer session, than to specify the question and answer each time because that method can cause the discussion to become disjointed. When Tony thought of something else I should know, not related to the question we were dealing with, he added it and it gets hard to organize his story into clear sections. I prefer to put his skills and his life story into categories and add my explanation of how this relates to what other mediums do.

Tony keeps a low profile because he wants his life to be simple and uncomplicated. He deals with only a few people he knows and only when the spirits of their loved ones ask him to make contact, when they have a message to pass on. He will occasionally get intuitions about people who are going to get ill or die and passes on the information if he thinks they can change something to avoid it. That falls into a realm that is almost clairvoyant, but he does not call himself that. He does not even want to receive this information, as this puts him in a difficult position.

He says there can be emotional overload, and there are days he wishes that no psychic or mediumistic information would come to him. The information comes spontaneously; he doesn't have to sit and meditate and say a prayer as most mediums do. On one occasion, Tony had to pull his car over because he was getting a message from Jordan. It is highly unusual to find a medium who can get messages so naturally – it demonstrates a highly connected brain at work, one very tuned to the spiritual plane. I am certain this is why he can get such amazing information, especially from Jordan, who has shown more than once that he can contact a medium at will, though he does so only when necessary.

Tony has no interest in acting as a medium for financial gain, since he feels his abilities are a gift from God to be used freely and not just restricted to those who can afford to pay for his services. I describe Tony as a top-level medium, because with his abilities he proven to me that an afterlife, which I had not previously believed in, does indeed exist and that Jordan is there, front and centre.

Many mediums do what they do because they truly want to use their gift to relieve people's grief and suffering. Research from the Institute for Applied Research in Human Potential, led by Dr. Julie Beischel, a top, well-qualified paranormal and afterlife researcher, which follows proper scientific protocols, proved that sessions with legitimate mediums reduce grief. There are scales like the Hamilton Anxiety Rating Scale and the Beck Depression Inventory that measure these conditions. I assume there are similar scales for grief, and many health professionals who work in collaboration with the Windbridge Institute, the centre where Dr. Beischel does her research, are skilled in using these.

Tony will not do mediumship full-time because he doesn't like all the baggage that comes with advertising one's services as a medium, and this does not allow him to help as many people as he otherwise could. A more important reason he avoids doing mediumship full-time is that he could damage his health by doing several readings a day. Even doing this sporadically, gathering information from sources few people can access can be a curse. He said to me, "Sometimes I just want it all to stop and be normal and have my brain to myself."

His life isn't easy. As I said, he is constantly bombarded by spirit communications, and as his former physician, I can state that he suffers from no mental illnesses that would cause him to make up imaginary things. These voices he perceives do not fit any of the criteria for schizophrenia or schizoaffective disorder. He displays some common issues with anxiety and occasional depression.

Tony is most distressed by his gift when he has difficulty staying in the moment and speaking to one spirit at a time. Some spirits are restless. They only want the opportunity to be heard for good reasons: to reassure their grieving loved ones that they exist and that a glorious reunion is just waiting to happen. Some other spirits have the same motivation but refuse to wait in line.

Great mediums John Edward and George Anderson have frequently said they have had to tell the spirits to wait their turn. I don't think I would have the courage to tell a spirit something like that, but then again if I saw a ghost, I would be scared as hell.

But given the constant psychic pressure, Tony is quite stable mentally and emotionally. There have been accomplished people in history who have heard voices, but from everything I have read, for instance about Joan of Arc, I don't think she was using mediumistic talents when she heard voices. The voices Tony hears are not random voices threatening him or telling him to do damaging things. They are not anonymous troublemakers originating from any kind of brain disease. The spirits identify themselves.

Tony Arpa was born in Toronto, Ontario. He later moved to Guelph, where he lived across the street from a woman named Kimberly Molto. Kimberly later received a Ph.D. in cognitive neuroscience, and she recognized his abilities at a young age. She describes them in one of her books.

Tony reports that his earliest memories are from when he was a baby. Remembering being a baby isn't usual, but it's not unheard of. He remembers his embryonic development, his birth, and his infancy. Although this sounds to me like a far-fetched claim, he's not the only person who has made it. Other people have reportedly experienced the same thing.

Tony has a non-mediumistic gift as well, which became apparent as a young child. It is best described as remote seeing. At age five, he told a teacher that JFK had just been shot. She scolded him, but a few minutes later the word got around the school from the radio, and Tony was under the impression that he was being made to feel responsible by thinking such a thing. This negative experience led Tony to keep the unusual things he experiences to himself. On top of being a medium, and showing clairvoyant ability, this ability makes Tony a triply-blessed person

People simply do not know what to do with children with psychic abilities. These kids get labelled as fanciful daydreamers, or worse, they're diagnosed with a mental illness. Some even get blamed for causing the negative events they correctly predict.

Tony sometimes knew something unusual was happening or was going to happen, but the hostile reaction he got from adults around him when he spoke up about it shattered his confidence and trust in people, so he often kept quiet. George Anderson's stories of his childhood in school are similar. In fact, a lot of mediums discover their unusual abilities in childhood but learn that they are not acceptable to others and actively try to suppress them.

Tony Arpa has made amazing contacts with the afterlife throughout his life, and he has shared many messages with their intended recipients. No medium fully understands their gifts at first, and as an adult, many years ago, he joined the Psychic Society of Toronto to learn more from experienced mediums. John Edward and George Anderson have reported that they had to join similar groups to fully understand what they needed to do to improve the use of their gifts.

Tony usually has spontaneous intermittent contact, and only sometimes does he have to sit down with someone for a reading. He does not do psychic life readings. He gets glimpses into people's futures, particularly about their health.

Tony was working full-time in a factory for quite a while, but he had to stop working after he was rear-ended at stoplights six times, and his back became too damaged to work. Dr. Beischel has looked closely at mediums for health problems and found that they have a far higher probability of having to deal with chronic illness than non-psychics. Tony has multiple sclerosis and other mediums suffer from autoimmune diseases like lupus, among other chronic medical conditions. Tony is now retired but doesn't want to do readings too frequently.

His contact with Jordan is unlike anything I have ever seen, and it is my firm belief that if Tony wants, he has the ability to be well-known, respected, and not at all susceptible to being debunked. I already described his statements to me, which he made without me going to see him or initiating contact with him. I reviewed our interactions in the interview to ensure that my timeline was correct and to validate his memory of what he said. I gave him the times and he repeated the messages. I have described them before, so I will be really brief here as a summary.

Tony's contact with Jordan all started when he received information about Jordan's lyric book and called me about it. He called a number of times with messages when I didn't expect anything, and he passed on a lot of information he could never have known by earthly means, especially the location of Jordan's guitars and the unusual electric and electronic malfunctions that only stopped when I really believed that Jordan was communicating with us. I came to believe over a period of fewer than two months. When I began acting as a believer should and stopped my constant harping on the fact that a lot of the things that were happening could be explained as just another unusual, but not paranormal, occurrence, all the electronic mayhem stopped.

Evidence like the phone calls on Jordan's second death anniversary and the incident in the coffee shop, when Tony was able to identify a friend of Jordan's, just kept coming, and I now accept that Tony is an excellent conduit for Jordan to use to keep passing information to me.

In Jordan's case, communications happened far earlier than usual; it may have been the combination of a highly-attuned brain and a strong spirit with an urgent need to reassure those he loved that caused this to be the exception to the rule. I had mentioned that Tony got a message from Jordan while driving and had to pull over to call me. This phone call was to let me know that Jordan had crossed over on day six. My subsequent investigations suggest that one may have to spend a few days in the astral plane, just below the higher plane of the true afterlife, to do a life review. Because it's possible that Jordan contributed to his own death, this makes sense to me now. Mediums often present evidence that suggests that some deceased people do their life review immediately after death.

Nothing is certain about our knowledge of something as multifaceted and obscure as the afterlife, except that information is constantly coming from that plane, outside of space and time.

I may have given the impression that I do nothing more in my contact with Tony than receive phone calls, but I have visited him on several occasions, as he is now my friend and no longer my patient.

Tony had been to my former house, where Jordan lived most of his life, only twice. He dropped by my house once well over a year after Jordan had died. It was a bit unusual: he rang the doorbell, but I had long since refused to answer my doorbell if I was not expecting someone over, so he went into the backyard and called to me. He said Jordan had told him that if he did that, I would answer and greet him. Around that time, the summer after Jordan died, I often refused to answer my phone, and I would check who had called only when I felt that I could stand to talk to people. Tony knew that calling me wasn't going to work either. He called out from the backyard, and I answered. He had no specific message that day; we just sat on the back porch and talked.

The second time he came over was when I had sold the house and had completely emptied it out. He came over the day before the new owner took possession, and we stood in the empty basement. He pointed to where Jordan had kept some of his things, like his bed and TV – and he was correct. He said Jordan was no longer spending time in the house, and that he would only come around where I was. At that time, five days before Christmas, I was in the hospital in a long inpatient program for severe depression and in grief and loss therapy. I had gotten only a short pass, allowing me to leave for a few hours to deal with closing the house and removing the last few small things. And although friends and family members had taken care of clearing out the house, selling that house was still a huge burden to me, especially while I was in the hospital. I was relieved to just go back to the hospital for Christmas, where my mood and my interaction with people was the best it had been since Jordan died. I have often wondered if that is why I may – and I stress the word *may* – have been able to have some interaction with Jordan on Christmas Day. I had not felt Jordan's presence in eighteen highly-stressful months, but that day I felt at peace.

I have visited Tony at his home three or four times, but we never sat down for a formal mediumistic reading. We usually just talked, but on one occasion when I had got another short pass from the hospital to visit him, he told me as soon as I stepped in the door that Jordan had brought another spirit with him – the young man his age I mentioned before. I specifically asked him if he was seeing a vision of Jordan and this other person, but he said he does not usually *see* spirits, instead getting the information in his brain.

I have asked every medium I have seen if they could see an apparition of Jordan. They all said they could not, that their mediumship didn't work like that. I am, and I am sure other people are, curious about this because quite a few mediums say that they actually see forms and describe their appearance in detail. One of these mediums is George Anderson, who says that this happens when a spirit really wants to be recognized, and the medium can later confirm this kind of contact by correctly picking out the person from a collection of similar photographs.

Healing

Tony has said he can sometimes heal injuries, but not major illnesses, and in the last chapter, I will describe how I seem to have done a similar thing once. Tony tells me that he has healed people by touch, but I can't confirm this, and cannot get details from the people he has helped because these people are not easily available for me to speak with. Partly, I didn't bother to track down the people he healed because although I agreed to write a book, I didn't agree to run all over hell's half acre to do research for it. The information I had to wade through was enough. I do not intend to take on the job of investigative reporter – other people get paid to do that; I don't.

Remote Viewing

Tony has had two episodes of seeing a death as it happened: the shooting of JFK and a more recent incident where he saw, somewhere in his brain, an acquaintance being murdered in Germany. He later learned that these deaths were actually happening at the time he saw them. This ability is hard to classify. The mechanism of how that works is not clear. These may not have anything to add to the evidence of the afterlife. It seems that perhaps a dying brain can send out a general distress signal and some people have the ability to receive that signal.

Clairvoyance

Tony has foreseen disasters and has told others, but much like John Edward, these come as a sense of unease, without specifics to warn people. Tony's ex-father-in-law was a chief firefighter, and Tony told him about warnings he was getting, more like vague premonitions, involving an upcoming need to rescue people from tall buildings on fire. He asked his father-in-law, Gord, who has now passed on, to look into seeing if there were new ways he could come up with of rescuing people from tall buildings, as his premonition was strong, and he got it just a few months before the twin towers were attacked in 2001. He had assumed it was something that was going to happen in Guelph, where there aren't any really tall buildings. Of course, Gord wanted more details, but Tony couldn't provide them any more than John Edward could for the extremely disturbed feelings he had before 9/11. John Edward described this in one of his books, and said it was far more disturbing than any other feeling of foreboding he had ever gotten. A lot of people have been reported sensing 9/11 but not having details.

Tony has as many talents as anyone I have read about or heard of, and at such high levels that it makes him an unusually gifted, multitalented psychic and medium. But those gifts are not the focus of this book. To get back to the book's core purpose, the purpose of providing the best evidence of the afterlife, I have to point out the validating aspects, provided by not one, but four different mediums living in four different cities.

Tony has been a key in this. Three of the mediums did not know each other. The fourth, Alfina, had not spoken to Tony in many years. A spirit like Jordan giving similar information to different mediums is some kind of added proof that this is real. There was also different information given at different times that showed that he was aware of what was going on in our lives – more good evidence. Four validations are always more powerful than just one.

I have written this chapter to thank Tony. I also want to think Jordan for reaching out and finding Tony to relay his messages to, and to thank the other mediums I met with for their efforts to provide me with evidence that my son is still doing well in another place. I also want to let you, the reader, know that Jordan is not a unique case. The people who have left you in this life are also doing just fine in the afterlife.

THREE

How to Tell a Bad Medium from a Good One in Under Ten Minutes

Some frauds who call themselves psychic mediums have no medium abilities but have read up on how to pull off a con job, while others have some weak talents but haven't taken the time or put in the effort to learn how to interpret the faint, unclear messages they get, and they guess instead. It's hard to figure out which mediums are good and which are faking it by looking them up in the phone book, but if there are psychic fairs in your town, go ask as many people as possible which mediums they think are good. People who have been burned are going to be happy to enlighten you.

One note of caution about psychic fairs: most psychics aren't mediums. If you want to connect with the deceased, it's not going to happen through tea-leaf readings. Psychics mostly offer life advice, but if you want to talk to a loved one you've lost, advice is not what you need. These psychics will only help you if what you're wondering is if you're going to get a job promotion or find a new soulmate, or what colours of clothing are going to bring you good luck. You can look for mediums online, but watch out for websites that list the ten best mediums in the city who are all at the same address. That's not a good sign. One or two mediums in a medium mill may be good, but there's no way all ten are legit.

You can look at the websites of individuals or businesses and review their offerings. If mediumship is far down the list of what they offer – under reiki treatment, love advice, dog walking – chances are they don't offer good mediumship. However, if someone is a medium, and a medium only, they might be worth looking into. Also note that testimonials can be suspect. Don't believe everything on the medium's website.

Some mediums offer group sessions at a much lower price than a full reading. Going to a group session is a good way to do a test run on a medium. Your departed may not come through in a large group session, since everyone's needs are present, but you can see how the medium works and if they seem successful in communicating with spirits in the afterlife. You can book a solo reading with the mediums who impress you.

If the group session doesn't work out, try it out with someone else. You may get lucky like I did with two of my five mediums and your loved one will do the work for you by directly intervening with a medium they trust. That medium will then find you.

I was fortunate to have friends in the know, whose advice turned out to be good. (Except in the one case where I accepted second-hand information.) If possible, find someone you know who has been to the medium you're interested in seeing. An honest medium will tell you that they don't control what spirits come through. If possible, ask questions about how they get messages, and if you find one that tells you your loved one appeared to them when you called, you have hit the jackpot.

If you run into a fake, after the precautions I will mention, just leave as soon as it becomes apparent that no evidential information is coming through. If you are told that the psychic channels an entity, then claims that your loved one will speak through the channel, forget it. Much better to go with a medium who contacts the deceased directly.

A friend of mine recommended my first medium after Tony. They knew someone who had seen her. That was my first mistake. I did not ask the actual client who had been to see the medium. If I had, I would never have wasted the time and money. I also did not ask what the fees were upfront, and if the session would be for a specific time. The medium started out by getting me to sign a waiver that I was not going to act on any advice, especially medically. I should have refused to sign it to see what would happen. Fake mediums have you sign a waiver so they don't get sued for telling you nothing, or garbage.

When she then told me she channelled the Elohim, I was

disturbed, but I hung in, as I was there already, and I figured it would at least be a learning experience. The Elohim are mentioned 2,500 times in the Bible and I had to wonder what they had been doing between that time and when she started her business. She asked me why I was there – she's the psychic with a team of gods backing her up and she had to ask.

I just slid my son's death card on the table. It had Batman on the front. She started in on a discussion about Batman and what I thought he meant to Jordan. She managed to milk that conversation for thirty minutes. During that time, I asked twice, about fifteen minutes apart, where the Elohim were from, suggesting two different places. She said yes to both (short-term memory apparently suffers when you're concentrating on dragging out a session for more money). After half an hour, I got fed up and asked to speak to Jordan.

She finally brought the entities into play, by looking up at the ceiling. I looked too, and saw nothing, not even a bit of transparent being. I assumed they were in the attic, or on the roof. Apparently, they told her to tell me that Jordan was angry because I wasn't taking the irrelevant Batman discussion seriously. I told her that I understood that the spirit plane was void of negative emotions like anger. I think she thought I was being a smart-ass, and may have gotten a bit upset, but that did not throw her off at all.

She said that Jordan was saying he had not done all his tasks in life (maybe a bit too obvious, since he died at twenty-two years old). She was being told that he wanted me to finish them for him, so I asked what tasks. She glanced at the ceiling again and said he wanted justice done. (She had gone on for ten minutes on how Batman stood for justice.) I could have told her that I did not have all of Batman's stuff, not even a cape, but I just said I don't see how I could do that vigilante action, as I did not have a gun, and it had been forty years since I was a martial arts champion. In the shape I was in, I could no longer fight; I had pulled a hamstring just photocopying, so fighting wasn't going to happen.

I had read in a *Reader's Digest* about how to spill the beans on fake mediumship. Fake mediums would usually first get into a general discussion, and when pressed, give generic answers. They would then move on to flattering the client, so they didn't ask specific questions about their loved one. Well, I had just stepped right into the trap by mentioning martial arts. I had handed her an opening. She went right for it, telling me I was a champion because I knew what my opponent would do a second before he did it. I could not resist pointing out that was exactly what Qui-Gon Jinn had said to Anakin Skywalker's mother in *Star Wars Episode I*, and that was a Jedi trait. She actually said the Force was strong with me. I was so surprised, that I forgot to ask her to ask the Elohim to materialize a light sabre for me.

I am not going to detail the rest of the nonsense (apparently my name had sacred vibrations, and I was capable of doing anything). This had gone on way too long, and her friends on the ceiling were obviously nowhere near Jordan, as I am sure he wisely skipped the session, knowing that he could not possibly connect with someone with no mediumship ability. She went through a charade of cleansing my energy by moving her hands up and down, both front and back, and had the nerve to tell me that Jordan was two feet behind me, but moved to two feet in front when she started drawing negative energy from my back. He was remarkably nimble and active when dodging bad energy.

I badly needed a cigarette, so I told her I was going outside for five minutes. I had the crystal skull bottle in the car, and I wanted to give her one last chance to redeem herself. I showed it to her and asked her to ask her friends what the symbols were. After a few seconds staring at the ceiling, she said she was told it was an arrow. I told her it was a happy face, and I asked if they had a clue where Jordan was.

She changed the subject by telling me she had a skull like that from Atlantis. She had held a ceremony with it in her barn, during which people were cured of illnesses. I had read about a scam artist in the area making money showing a crystal skull she claimed to have found in Belize in the 1920s. I gave her the name of the woman, and she was shocked that I knew it. I then explained that the skull had been proven to be a total fake.

That was it. The session was over. She said she charged $150 per hour, and the session was over two hours, so the fee was $400. I had $300 on me, so I gave that to her and walked out. I consider it payment for learning about fake mediums and channellers, and it gave me material for this book, so I am not complaining. I told the person who had suggested that I see her, and she was so angry that she told other people. The fake's website no longer lists her as a medium or channeller.

Try these strategies to help you avoid getting scammed by fake mediums:

1. Question the person who saw the medium.
2. Don't sign any form, and see what they do.
3. As soon as they bring channelling into it, leave.
4. If they ask why you are there, remind them they are psychic and they should know.
5. Watch for pointless discussions that waste time.
6. If you don't get one bit of specific validation after a half hour, interrupt the flattery and ask why.

Don't give up on mediums because of a bad experience. There are good ones out there.

Many mediums have been shown on TV to be fakes. They were caught using the tricks that skeptics accuse them of. Don't let that put you off mediums; these are not ones you are likely to see. You need a neighbourhood medium. If I could dig, ask around and find good ones, you can too.

And when you read total garbage in books by mediums, and channellers, just ignore them, they do not represent the good mediums who want to use their gifts to help people. Not every medium book is bad, but the ones that fill up a shelf at a thrift store are often the useless ones people could not wait to give away. You also have to judge for yourself if what you are reading sounds realistic or ridiculous. It can help you know what to expect from a good medium.

Good Mediums

There are many honest, reliable mediums. I will share what I have found out to help anyone tell when a medium is legitimate.

A medium who charges a lot is either in high demand because they are top-flight or they are just in it for the money. If they have a long wait-list, it means people are coming back, or a lot of new people want to see them because they are good. In Canada, the average rate for a medium is $150 for one hour.

If the fee is acceptable, and you want to see that medium, you may want to ask first if you can have a shorter session. Thirty minutes is enough sometimes. In my experience, spirits don't hang around for more than an hour, so don't run up extra overtime charges, unless you are totally blown away by the information coming through.

Your loved ones tend to know you are coming, and show up before you walk in the door. If that happens, you likely have found a good medium.

Even a good medium may not be able to get the one specific person you want right off the bat. Someone else may show up, and if the information is valid, wait a few minutes and ask if the person you want to see is there. Sometimes, a spirit who is new to communicating has to watch how another spirit does it before trying.

You can ask for a quick explanation about how the medium is receiving the messages – by voice, images, or thoughts. A good medium will tell you, while a fake may flounder, especially if you ask a follow-up question. Be careful not to interrupt a good spirit reading to do this; wait until after the session.

Try not to get into long episodes of questions and answers, and don't volunteer information. Many mediums described in books operate by asking yes or no questions. My mediums, however, tell me things I can confirm or deny. Often I don't need to interject at all, and the information just flows. At that point, I only need to ask for clarification. Consider the information the medium gives you. Would the information provided be hard for someone to guess or do you suspect that the medium is just drawing logical conclusions from information they have about you?

If you aren't sure contact was made because the information isn't specific enough and doesn't reflect what only the deceased would know, then look for someone else. You absolutely need that validation.

Make sure you get a direct validation medium and not a channeller. Also, watch out for people who are psychic but who aren't mediums.

If the same person does other things in addition to mediumship, like hypnotic past life regressions, try to pick someone else.

I am wary when the medium and partners sell goods like crystals and offer other services that are not directly related to contacting the dead, such as give workshops.

The bottom line here is to use good judgment, and try not to let grief blind you to inconsistencies in a medium's interaction with you. Most of us deep down can tell when someone is honest and sincere, so listen to your intuition.

PART 2

Research on the Afterlife – Studies and Opinions

FOUR

Researching the Afterlife

I didn't want to write a book like this because it feels too much like writing a science paper, and it's a lot of work.

But after getting such clear evidence of the afterlife from my son, I knew I had to write this book. And if I don't, who will? So I honour my son, and I push on.

I outline below the types of evidence to look for in a contentious topic like this.

Scientific Evidence

Gathering scientific evidence involves following scientific protocols to complete well-planned experiments and then analyzing the evidence properly to reach a valid conclusion. Good studies on the afterlife have been carried out at the University of Arizona by Dr. Gary Schwartz, and the Windbridge Institute's founder, Dr. Julie Beischel, has carried the research forward with stricter protocols. These studies have been attacked with little reason. The Forever Family Foundation has done a small, limited study in this area. Dr. Ian Stevenson has done extensive research on children who show evidence of past lives, and some scientists are starting to do experiments with technology to capture voices, images, and messages from the afterlife on recording equipment.

There is ever-increasing scientific evidence on the side of afterlife proponents, with every medium study, every validated contact with those who have transitioned, and even with every complete near death experience (NDE) report. The biggest controversy is about whether medium studies that are done using scientific methods can be called scientific. I believe they fit the criteria, and I accept them as scientific.

Anti-afterlife advocates draw conclusions from the results of various studies to support their position. These experiments were not often done to refute the anti-afterlife hypothesis. There is a bit of scientific evidence that is put forward as evidence of the nonexistence of the afterlife; this is mostly meta-analysis, which involves going back and looking at previous scientific data and trying to bring it to bear on this issue. A few new experiments have been done to try to disprove the reality of NDEs, and I address that below.

James Randi, an ex-magician who is committed to disproving mediums' abilities, has formed what some claim is a valid research organization called the Committee for Skeptical Inquiry (CSI). One of CSI's stated goals is to do research to disprove the afterlife; however, in forty years, not one proper research study has been done. Randi suggests that their work is scientific when they do things like point out what is wrong with mediums and attack actual scientific experiments. Randi has also organized hoaxes to draw press attention by having fake mediums infiltrate studies, like sending a fake guru to Australia. For years, his fans have touted a travesty called The Million Dollar Challenge, which many, who have analyzed the conditions set down, state is nothing but a cynical publicity stunt, rigged so no challenger has anything approaching a fair chance of getting any money. These plants serve CSI as "experiments" to prove that mediums are frauds, that there is no afterlife, and that the public is gullible. This is not scientific research, it is attention-seeking, and it does not provide evidence of anything to do with the afterlife.

Objective Evidence

This refers to real objects, or events, recorded and analyzed, that can be provided as proof for, or against, an argument.

However, in the case of the afterlife, neither believers nor deniers have anything that is acceptable to the other.

Stories of spiritual replicas leaving dying bodies have been reported by many, but no verifiable photographs have been taken.

There are reports that nurses in Brazil have witnessed this phenomenon so often that they treat it as routine. One photograph would be all that's needed to prove that this happens – and a video would be even better. However, hospitals make you turn your cellphones off and don't let you carry them into a room where a patient is dying, since that would be disrespectful. By the time you run to get the phone and turn it on, the spirit is gone. There are rumours that there have been pictures of these spirits taken in the former Soviet Union, but these are unsubstantiated.

The British medium Leslie Flint, along with Betty Greene and George Woods, created a large collection of recordings made during seances starting in the 1950s. While tied to a chair and blindfolded with his mouth taped, Flint acted as the medium for the spirit's direct voice, which came through an ectoplasmic voice box. Some voices taped reportedly sounded like the communicator, which was verified by those who knew the spirit. These recordings have never been seriously mentioned as objective evidence of the afterlife. It may be because the audio equipment wasn't great and the setting of the seances was unsupervised. I listened to several of these recordings online, but I was not impressed. None of the spirits said anything important, and it could have been a ventriloquist doing accents. There was no verifiable information, nothing that only someone in the afterlife would know.

There are a few reports of spirit communication captured on computers, but again, the evidence is slim.

The most convincing evidence from the much-quoted Scole Experiment is spirit-imprinted images and poems on unopened rolls of film that were supposedly guarded from start to finish (see my description of these experiments in the next chapter). However, there are suggestions that sleight of hand may have been used somewhere in this process to artificially impress images on film.

All of the above is tenuous, at best, objective evidence to prove that the afterlife exists. The safest thing to do, for the sake of credibility, is to say there is no objective evidence that both sides will ever agree with.

Anecdotal Evidence

Anecdotal evidence includes verbal or written reports from individuals about things they've seen or heard. You can find anecdotal evidence not only in informal conversations with people, but also in some neuroscience reports, which involve listening to what patients say concerning how they feel.

Many reliable people have given well-analyzed reports about their NDEs, which allude to an afterlife, and there are a lot of scientists now involved in doing rigorously-controlled interviews to collate this anecdotal data. Deniers dismiss these experiences as hallucinations.

There are hundreds of thousands of reports of mediums connecting with the deceased. These reports offer impressive validation that something real is happening, but again skeptics dismiss them as fraudulent.

Skeptics would do well to heed the words of Carl Gustav Jung. He said in 1919, in a speech to the Society for Psychical Research in England, "I shall not commit the fashionable stupidity of regarding everything I cannot explain as a fraud." Nearly one hundred years later, Jung's quote still rings true, describing how anti-afterlife advocates don't really disprove the afterlife. They simply dismiss it because they can't explain it.

Anecdotal evidence is acceptable in a court of law, especially if it is corroborated by similar evidence from others. It is high time all the evidence was gathered up and presented as evidence.

Sources

Books

There are different types of books on mediumship:

- mediums writing about themselves. (I have read many of these to get an idea of what value they have as proof of the afterlife.)
- authors writing about one or more mediums. The best example I found was *We Don't Die: George Anderson's Conversations with the Other Side*.

- authors writing about experiments they've completed on the afterlife or mediumship. These are well accepted by most, but there are also some opponents who are loud in their criticisms.

- authors writing about a range of topics like the nature of after-death communications, life plans made by souls planning to reincarnate, and some exploring past lives.

- authors writing about popular spiritual gurus. These books tend to contain a lot of claims but provide little evidence.

- NDE survivors writing about their experiences.

- researchers and analysts of paranormal phenomena looking for proof of the afterlife, or at least trying to show that the consciousness of a person can survive intact outside of the body.

- deniers writing to disprove the afterlife. There are not that many examples of this, but included among them is one 675-page effort, claiming to prove that the afterlife does not exist.

I did only a little research on religious scriptures, ancient or modern, because the reliability of these giving a correct picture of the afterlife is undermined by the fact that these scriptures tend to disagree with each other.

Journal articles

Dr. Julie Beischel from the Windbridge Institute and several others on that team, as well as other NDE researchers claiming evidence for the afterlife, publish in journals. Most of these are journals dealing with parapsychology, but I know of at least one of their articles making it into a highly respected medical journal, *The Lancet*.

Internet articles

There is a lot of information online about the afterlife, and it gets tiring to wade through it. Google gives over five million hits when you search "afterlife." Finding anti-afterlife sites and articles is difficult since most sites are pro-afterlife and the anti-afterlife arguments are buried, except on Wikipedia, where the bias against this belief is extreme. In fact, I gave up looking for them after a few days of painfully dredging out information I could use. There are quite a few sites run by religious organizations, but I stuck to the principle that these likely had biases.

Dedicated websites

Afterlife TV with Bob Olson is wide ranging. Olson interviews a varied group of authors, doctors, a lot of NDE survivors, and mediums. They discuss everything to do with the afterlife, including how to plan for the next life, and the interviewees often provide detailed descriptions of the afterlife. It's not a bad place to start, but I had to be very alert and selective about the information I got from there.

Dr. Elisa Medhus, whose son Erik committed suicide at age twenty, runs the blog *Channelling Erik*. She uses several mediums who get information from Erik on a wide range of topics and who get Erik to access spirits in the afterlife, including Jesus, murderers, celebrities, and scientists. "Erik, on the physics of death" was an interesting post. Dr. Medhus has written a couple of books related to the afterlife, including *My Life After Death: A Memoir from Heaven*, in which Erik describes his life, death, and all that has happened since. The information in the book was relayed through mediums, and it was written by his mother. The actual reports of the afterlife can't be verified, but it offers a perspective about that plane that makes more sense than much of the other information out there.

Tony told me that Jordan wanted me to go on the *Channelling Erik* site. Tony claimed he hadn't heard of the site before. I corresponded with Elisa, and she was quite gracious. She suggested that Jordan and Erik nudged me to go on that site.

You can find a lot of good information on real science on the web if you search with intent. I used several of these sites to evaluate the validity of arguments on both sides. Many sites are in the form of blogs, some are research papers. On valuable sites like Paranormalia, and skeptiko.com, you can find intelligent discussion among seemingly intelligent people on a wide variety of issues.

The websites run by skeptics seem to have a more aggressive tone, and they become repetitive in calling people who speak up in favour of the afterlife idiots and liars.

YouTube

You can find some fairly informative videos on YouTube about the afterlife, including TED talks by Dr. Stuart Hameroff and Dr. Fred Alan Wolf, which go into some good afterlife science.

The deniers also get their turn on YouTube. There are many sites that claim there is proof, both for and against the afterlife. Many are religious sites, and they use scripture and philosophy in their arguments. Some sites at first appear to be a long series of apparently neutral investigators, trying to find out the evidence for and against the afterlife. In the end, the evidence usually comes down to the opinion of the commentator, and I get the impression that their mind was made up before they asked their first question. They also never appeared to take mediumship seriously, only interviewing scientists, philosophers, and theologians – all with obvious biases.

FIVE

Evidence for the Afterlife

I truly believe that I have been given overwhelming, unassailable evidence of the afterlife. The evidence proves that at least my son and several others continue to exist after death. But this proof is merely personal. It convinces me, but it may not convince you.

I do not use the word *proof* often, especially when referencing science. I realize that the word *proof* can only apply to mathematics and liquor. Science, by definition, is applicable only when there is a law, theory, or hypothesis that is falsifiable. My proof is not scientific, as science cannot deal with ultimate truths. So, rather than give you proof, I'll supplying an overwhelming amount of evidence to the point that the afterlife cannot be doubted (a bit unwieldy compared to just calling it *proof*).

I guess I had better start delivering on my statements above. I was quite extensive in my research, but it would take many years to cover all the evidence, so I offer you my best effort.

We Don't Die: George Anderson's Conversations with the Other Side

George Anderson is considered by many to be the gold standard of mediumship in the world.

After life-threatening encephalitis at age six, George began to see spirits, and sometimes knew when someone would die. When he talked about what he was seeing and hearing in Catholic school, the nuns diagnosed him as either demon-possessed or schizophrenic. The nuns made the irrational decision to send him to an asylum instead of following church protocol, which requires calling in a priest to do an exorcism. That didn't happen, but it would have been awesome if they sprinkled holy water on him and he screamed, "It burns. It burns." The nuns, priests, and kids would have run faster than Usain Bolt, suffering groin strains, hamstring pulls, and other assorted injuries.

George's biography is available online, so you can find more information about his life if you're interested. It's enough for our purposes to know that he kept his mouth shut from then on, then as an adult he started using these abilities, that he did not understand, in a limited way.

Radio host Joel Martin has a reputation as a psychic debunker. His staff had heard of George and pestered him until he agreed to see him. Joel's agenda was to debunk George, but then the unexpected happened: George gave such stunning information to Joel, a stranger, that the skeptic was astonished. This included information about Joel's grandfather, a very religious Jewish man, who told George that the proudest day of his life was Joel's bar mitzvah and the saddest was the day he left the faith. Joel stated he had never publicized any of this and that this was not documented anywhere. He also was able to tell Joel that his wife, who had been killed in a car accident years before, thought he was too lenient on his daughter. George could exactly mimic her posture and the hand gestures she had used regularly in her lifetime. This was enough to make Joel start having doubts about his skepticism.

Joel arranged for another committed skeptic to have a reading done by George over the phone. He had no prior notice of who this person was, and only a first name was used. George gave a great deal of personal information to the sitter, verifiable things that he could not have known. He told this man that someone close to him had severe heart problems and asked repeatedly if it was a very close relative or friend. He kept getting no answers until the caller said that he himself was the one with the bad heart. This shows no medium is perfect, but he was giving specific detailed information he could not have guessed and had stuck to his guns. He did not think of the possibility that his afterlife contact meant the caller himself when he said it was someone who was very, very close. This shows that a medium can get great information from the other side, but they have to interpret it themselves. This was another totally mind-blowing session that convinced Joel of George's connection with the afterlife. Joel then wanted to share George's talents with his listeners.

George was shy and had to be convinced to do readings on Joel's radio show. He did readings by phone, which were incredible. He then started doing more personal readings.

We Don't Die was written by Joel Martin and Patricia Romanowski, a journalist working for Toronto publications (which is instant credibility in my mind, as I grew up in that fine city myself).

As described in the book, George continued to show a high degree of accuracy in his sessions, and a lot of the usual charges of fraud trotted out by debunkers could not be applied to this medium. In person, he asked for only yes-no answers, and barely looked at the sitters, mostly occupied with scribbling on a pad. At one point, a psychiatrist decided to trip him up, and showed up for the reading at George's home shabbily dressed and reeking of alcohol. George kept seeing an image of Freud above this man's head. In a situation where a lesser talent would be fooled into thinking he was dealing with someone of lower stature, he got the information about the sitter through persistent images.

Chapter one of *We Don't Die* jumps out at you, like I hope the first chapter here does. He correctly identified the spirit of a sixteen-year-old boy, popular with everyone, and a high school soccer star who had been killed by a hit-and-run driver. This spirit, David, was so strong and motivated that he showed himself to George, who in a later reading picked out his correct picture from among a group of similar looking kids. He was specific, highly accurate, and ended up doing four readings for different people all associated with David. The basics were reproducible, even though he only realized near the end of some readings that this was the boy he had contacted before. This confusion was understandable because much time had passed between readings, and George had done thousands of readings in-between. Different information was added in each session as David became aware of changes taking place over time in the lives of people who were still living.

Many of George's readings are absolutely mind-boggling. George Anderson is the real deal, and I don't see how anyone can doubt that he has been in contact with real entities from the spirit world. Unfortunately, he is prone to suffering the pain associated with a death he is describing, but it is not prolonged. And if he can prove that one or more persons live beyond death, it can be assumed that we all do.

George has given information that had not happened, a miss, but in one case the scenario he saw – a bend in a mountain road and a truck coming directly at the driver – happened to the sitter a few days later. Fortunately, the driver recognized the bend that had been described and pulled over just before the truck could hit him. He only could do only one experiment in the University of Arizona Veritas study due to prior commitments, but his score was so high that, in my opinion, all the criticism that the raters were scoring the accuracy of the readings too high, did not apply enough to invalidate the findings. His score could have dropped 20 percent, and still provided indisputable evidence that he spoke to the deceased.

I repeat, all it takes is one proven case in experimental conditions for the white raven or black swan theory to take effect and provide a fatal blow to debunkers. One black swan or white raven found disproves the assertion that there is no such thing as a black swan or a white raven. Similarly, one medium connecting with one spirit in the afterlife, is adequate grounds to blow the no-afterlife theory out of the water, hence the frenzied attack on any afterlife evidence by deniers using blatantly poor scientific judgment and knowledge, to try to nullify a done deal.

His high fees are being attacked today, but he is the best and has to have a large full-time staff to handle the demands for his time. He can only do limited readings a week, as they are mentally and physically taxing. This might suggest that as mediums get older their sustainable reading ability diminishes.

I am not saying that this is happening with George. I am only mentioning that, as I have been seeing some accusations that his readings are not as reliable, with one person deeming one absolutely terrible. It is the disgruntled that tend to post on the internet, and he has done over 30,000 readings, so a couple of bad posts to skeptic sites, does not invalidate a lifetime of valid work. He still is considered the best public medium in the world, and has done *more than enough to prove the existence of the afterlife*. To debunkers, I would say "Prove he is wrong, or admit that he has, all by himself, blown you out of the water."

Books by Other Mediums

Many books by mediums have been written, and while there is a lot of information in many of them that supports the afterlife, a few make mediumship a laughingstock. There are just too many coming out – more each month – for me to even try to read them all. John Edward has some good information on some verified readings he has done, where it really appears he is in contact with the afterlife. He has contacted many who passed on 9/11, and some of the specific personal information he gave as validation was very good.

Some other mediums considered good enough to be targeted by debunkers have written books. These include the Long Island Medium, Theresa Caputo (Anderson and Edward are also from Long Island – must be something in the water there), Allison Dubois, Lisa Williams, Sunny Dawn Johnston, John Holland, Maureen Hancock, Chip Coffey – basically every psychic that has ever been listed as a top-ten psychic in the United States gets to write a book (or several books). I read some, scanned some, looked some reviews up, and my impression is that stripped down, they're all the same book: different mediums in different situations, recounting many amazing readings, verified as true by the sitters.

How good is this as evidence for the afterlife? I got the impression that these accounts were about legitimate spirit communications, and there is strength in numbers as evidence of the afterlife. I think that if they were all frauds, they would have been called out by someone – other than the closed-minded, dyed-in-the wool skeptics who bash mediums on anti-afterlife websites and pat each other on the back for their rationality and intelligence. On those sites, all mediums and all their books are dismissed as fake.

These mediums are public figures, and their stories can be verified or debunked. While there are often a few comments online claiming that the medium's reading was wrong, it's usually surrounded by many other comments saying that the readings were accurate to the point that the person leaving the positive comment was convinced that no faking was going on.

Numbers of consistent reports are important in evaluating the probability of a thing being true. The more that mediums write about sessions they did in private and the more they provide recordings of proper readings, the more the evidence mounts. Mediums most often get criticized for readings where they try to contact spirits in the circus-like atmospheres of TV show sets. Good readings are recorded in their books, but there is likely a lot of difficulty with the deceased being able to send clear messages while being filmed for TV, and this is where the skeptics have a field day.

Not all books are of the calibre of those by the mediums considered to be the best around, at least among those who have a very public profile. James Van Praagh is still listed as a top-ten medium. I have read many of his books, and they were just okay. Instead of focusing on readings, he diverts to other things such as clearing a house of an evil, damaging spirit that was ripping the house apart and not allowing it to be built, as well as providing a lot of instructions on how readers can prepare themselves to contact the other side. I tried these methods, but they didn't work for me, and almost everything I read or see on the internet gives the same instructions. If I really believed that giving up caffeine would help me see my spirit guide, I would try. But then none of those techniques ever work for me (maybe because relaxation and freeing the mind are not in my vocabulary). These are not as convincing as books about mediums like George Anderson. Praagh may have been connected as a medium at one time, but recently he has been getting himself into situations that do not inspire confidence.

In fact, while Anderson is the most validated and tested public medium currently, Praagh is the most targeted and ridiculed medium alive today. Sylvia Browne had that distinction before she died in 2013. So far, I haven't heard of her making contact from the afterlife. While she was living, Browne asserted that she was far advanced as a soul and that she was going to one of the highest planes, so maybe in that plane contact with mere mortals is just not done.

Some mediums don't know when to say they aren't getting any messages, so they make up stories. Praagh and Browne ran into trouble because of this, and they fell flat on their faces as they got older. I can't find any reliable evidence of the effect of aging on mediumship. However, they are human, and there is evidence suggesting that mediums are more disease-prone than non-mediums, plus the painful effects of receiving messages may expedite deterioration of the mind and body. Two of the mediums I went to told me it took two or three days before they had the energy to get out of bed to do things after they spent a few hours doing readings with me.

Still, improvising and getting things wrong harms the reputation of all mediums, and thus the legitimacy of afterlife communications. Giving parents with missing children tragically wrong information, as Browne did twice on the Montel Williams show, was especially bad form.

Browne and Ruth Montgomery have published as much, if not more than, any other medium. Each of their books, however, is more farcical than the previous. I have a few issues with Browne's books, which I'll discuss later. Ruth Montgomery lost credibility with me when she described that the soul group she is in now has been together for millions of years, and were once busy fighting off dinosaurs in Lemuria. Some mediums' books are definitely not helping the case for the afterlife.

Rosemary Altea is something else, but I'm not sure what exactly. She has the ability to go through a tunnel in time to watch people die or get killed in fires as she stands next to the bereaved, in the presence of her spirit guide, Grey Owl.

Then there are books by people who have spoken to mediums (like this book, I guess). Bob Olson and Dr. Elisa Medhus get answers from the afterlife through many mediums, and they offer some useful information. Robert Schwartz and Dr. Michael Newton write about souls planning their next life on earth. This planning takes place in the afterlife, and both mediums use past life regressions, but they must get the person to stop jumping from life to life and chill out in the afterlife to give us their insight. Some of the advice makes sense, but I am not that interested in planning yet another life, as I am not in a hurry to come back.

So, are books involving mediums, and even past life regressions, good evidence for the existence of the afterlife? The quantity alone of verified readings that have not been debunked acts as great evidence. The books by mediums that were obviously suspect to begin with can be removed from the equation. There are always going to be people that will write books who should not have gone anywhere near a computer or typewriter. A bad book does not invalidate a good book, and certainly does not invalidate an entire field.

At the Hour of Death by Karlis Osis, Ph.D. and Erlander Haraldsson, Ph.D.

At the Hour of Death is well-researched and offers some additional arguments from a totally different body of suggestive evidence that may support the presence of the afterlife. The authors used over 1,000 doctors and nurses in India and the United States and got those who responded to provide detailed information on patients who had died, and indicated by their last words that they could see those in the afterlife coming to them. A few of the dying were scared, but most were peaceful. The spirits who had already passed were apparently communicating with the dying and helping them make the transition. These groundbreaking accounts add to the building evidence. This whole new angle helps corroborate the mediums' experience and creates a more airtight case for the afterlife.

Some of the patients who had a good prognosis died even though they weren't very ill. These are the most unexpected – and arguably the most important – pieces of data. The patients often told the medical staff they were going to die, which went against all the evidence that indicated they would soon be well. There were reports that they saw their double in white coming for them. It has long been reported that if a person sees their doppelgänger, they are going to die soon. That story may sound like folklore, and in ordinary circumstances, it probably is, but in these cases, these patients were in contact with something unexplained, and their information from that source seemed to be correct, which directly contradicted their medical circumstances.

The authors looked at every possible variable – age, pre-existing conditions, brain function impediments, medications, diagnosis from poor to good, religious and cultural issues, and attitudes on death. They did a chi-squared analysis and came up with a valid probability value for the hypothesis that these people were indeed seeing something. The probability value was calculated using multivariable analysis and their study performed a rigorous treatment of the data.

A lot of people die without saying anything, and sometimes people die while they're in a coma or asleep, but I don't see that this invalidates Osis and Haraldsson's look at how the afterlife interacts with us when people are in need at death's door.

Research by Dr. Julie Beischel – The Windbridge Institute

Dr. Beischel is probably the most active current researcher on the afterlife. In response to critics who had concerns about the validity of earlier double-blind studies, she is doing quadruple-blind studies.

The studies she conducts include readings in which the psychic was given only the name of the deceased that they were supposed to contact. Otherwise, the psychics gave their readings in the absence of the subjects of those readings. These people, the friends and family of the deceased, were sent multiple readings and rated them for how closely each reading applied to them. They were also asked to identify which reading was theirs. These studies put mediums in the most difficult circumstances, and Beischel has still obtained results with statistical significance that show there was real afterlife contact.

The researchers didn't do more than screen the medium to assess they had some credibility. They couldn't possibly have influenced the results. Surrogates picked the rest of the participants, and the mediums were not given anything that could be considered hints to help them.

About half the mediums were scored as accurate, compared to guessing, with a probability of less than 0.001 percent. These studies follow acceptable science protocols, and the results are valid. Dr. Beischel is criticized on skeptical websites, and of course she is going to be attacked by debunkers who are firm in their opinions against the afterlife and are not willing to look in detail at good results. No amount of data is going to satisfy them. One said that anything she studied was invalid because she believes mediumship exists. How ignorant is that? If they used such judgment in their work as scientists, they would lose all credibility.

When five or six out of eleven mediums tested reach that statistical probability mark that shows the results are likely honest – if you wanted to blow people away, you would somehow massage the data to get eleven of eleven. Only one proven case is all that's needed to tell deniers to get lost, but they still hang on to their opinions with no data to back them up and no good way to refute her data. They do what they do best – pretend it didn't happen or find some way to demonize her and everyone involved in the research. This kind of reaction is apparent in the next study I cite.

Research by Dr. Gary Schwartz – the VERITAS Program

There are many reasons for those interested in the afterlife to admire Dr. Gary Schwartz. He pioneered research into mediumship under laboratory conditions – and has been attacked and vilified for his trouble by James Randi's Committee for Skeptical Inquiry (CSI). Thankfully, Schwartz's book has outsold anything deniers write, so his work has been able to encourage many people.

The first experiment featured an all-star cast of mediums, including George Anderson, John Edward, Suzane Northrop, Reverend Anne Gehman, and one amateur, Laurie Campbell. The first part of the study featured a typical session with each medium, but where mediums were concealed from sitters. In this study, the mediums scored over 80 percent accuracy, with Anderson and Edward scoring the highest. In a later experiment, Dr. Schwartz acted as a go-between from sitter to medium, passing back and forth only yes or no answers so that inflections in voice could not be used in the reading. He was criticized for this on the grounds that a researcher should not be personally involved in his own study. Even though all he was doing was relaying answers from yes or no cards, his presence was not a good idea, and he corrected this in subsequent studies. In a later experiment, the mediums had to give information from a deceased relative or friend without asking questions of the sitter for the first half of the readings. They consistently proved accurate. However, Edward scored 0 percent for one sitter because the previous sitter's dead grandmother refused to leave, and he could not get through to the deceased associated with the current sitter.

Jordan did the same thing to one of my own all-star mediums, Mark. He interfered with his work until Mark gave me an urgent appointment, so Jordan could say what he wanted to say to me and Mark could get back to other work. I am so proud of that kid.

Later studies added elements like addressing rater bias and using proxy sitters, again where the subjects had to rate all the readings as they might apply to them, not just their own. The ratings of medium accuracy were lower in these situations, but they were still significant, as would be expected when the medium cannot get any feedback to allow them to elaborate on what a sitter would find most significant.

It cannot be stressed enough that the deceased has total control over what they give the medium. Spirits can't be prompted by the medium to go into more detail about any one topic, which cuts down on the amount of unique information they give. The deceased communicates with the medium, not the sitter. It's questionable if the deceased has the energy to deal with a medium and read the sitter's thoughts, since the sitters were not speaking directly with the medium and would not have their train of thought controlled by what they were hearing in real time. The accuracy was still significantly better than average, even with all the complexity, which would damage the level of communication. Some mediums see images around the sitter, and this valuable tool was taken away.

The results should have been acceptable to everyone; however, CSI's Dr. Ray Hyman tried to criticize the first study into oblivion. He said it was not double-blind. He is wrong; the mediums did not know who they were reading, and they were never allowed to see the sitters, who were selected by someone other than the researchers. Having no controls would mean that you have someone who is not a medium floundering around wasting time.

Another complaint about the experiments was about sensory leakage, where the medium picks up subtle signs from the sitter. Since the sitter was secluded and silent in the first half of one of the experiments, and yes-no answers were given by a neutral person, the sustained criticism was unwarranted. The mediums were still accurately coming up with brilliant gems of information. In all the conditions, they were coming up with dazzle hits, information that was detailed and could not be guessed. The medium Suzanne Northrop asked only five questions in a session where she came up with over thirty pieces of good information.

Dr. Hyman was quoted in the book as saying, "I do not control my beliefs." Even in the face of what can be described as overwhelming evidence, he was unable to accept even the compelling scientific data, and his beliefs had not changed.

Dr. Hyman observed one reading by John Edward where the medium produced thirty statements judged by the rater as accurately applying to her deceased father, saying they could apply to anyone. To prove his point, he showed that three of them could apply to his father. What about the other twenty-seven specific statements that did not apply to the critic's father? Dr. Hyman has been criticized by other scientists as being an inappropriate choice of critic for these studies, as he has been a committed denier for over forty years and is active in the anti-afterlife crusade. With this background, it would be difficult for anyone to be unbiased.

Schwartz's experiment was an astonishing success, with only some minor flaws in proper scientific protocol. However, even if you knock off a few points from the readings' accuracy, the scores were still high enough not to be guesses. These mediums were *actually talking to the deceased.*

This landmark study was by no means perfect. Most pioneering experiments aren't. Methods to make studies more and more valid come along as a field progresses.

One important point to remember is that resistance to the truth by skeptics does not invalidate the proof provided by these medium testing studies. The public, who are aware of these results, properly, believe real science when they see it. Surveys that took place in the 70s and recently suggest that belief in the afterlife has increased in the past few years. Religious adherence has dropped considerably in that time frame, so one cannot say that these beliefs are driven by religious fervour.

For those of you with strong beliefs in the afterlife, you are not alone, and with good reason.

I offer one final consideration of Dr. Schwartz's experiments: when skeptics attack the research, but their attacks fail, they then often attack the researcher in a smear campaign, as if doing so will change the result of the research. If you look up Dr. Schwartz online, you'll see that Geraldo Rivera "exposed" him as someone who tried to extort $3 million from a grieving father. I encourage you to look deeper. It was a set-up.

The fact that Dr. Schwartz is still in good standing at his university attests to the fact that he did nothing wrong. The only supposedly reliable place that accepts this fake story at face value is the extremely skeptically biased Wikipedia. They neglected to mention any of the details on Dr. Schwartz's side. There is a spirited debate online, with a lot of facts that ring true to me in favour of Dr. Schwartz. The website I got this from is dailygrail.com, where the facts were laid out piece by piece by someone in the know, and my impression of the opposition was that they just kept repeating that Dr. Schwartz was a fake, just like all the mediums he worked with.

Other centres, such as the University of Virginia, are doing research, but most of it is on NDEs. They offer tantalizing evidence but cannot prove the afterlife.

As I mentioned earlier, research like this is difficult to do. Dr. Schwartz was lucky to be part of an open-minded university. Dr. Beischel has had to open her own institute, funded by books published, donations, and other non-traditional funding. The researchers that are adamantly against any suggestion of an afterlife control much of the research funding. One prevailing theory is that it does not fit with their concepts of physics. If this connection between the earth plane and the afterlife dimension becomes more widely verified – and it is not clear how much more verification is needed – there would be pressure to do non-physical reality research.

Nikola Tesla, one of the brightest and most perceptive minds ever, suggested that incredible progress would be made in science if we tried to tap into the fields I mentioned in the last chapter. A lot of the work in research would have to change focus, and scientists are unwilling to do this for many reasons. It's really detrimental for everyone. I'm sure if we tapped into these fields, the whole energy economy of the world could change.

Electronic Voice and Computer Recordings

Professor Imants Barušs of the University of Western Ontario started analyzing recordings from static between radio stations a few years ago to see if spirits would try to communicate this way. Ghost hunters claimed they could see and hear ghosts in TV static. A few words may have been heard, but there was no spectacular evidence.

Barušs's group followed up by using a computer with a random word generator, with a medium present, to see if a spirit would respond by influencing the random words to make sense when a question was asked. There were some interesting short sentences heard as the medium kept asking what could be done to improve communication. They later asked eleven questions. The computer answered eight of eleven correctly, but while barely statistically significant, it was not used as evidence of communications by way of electriconic voice recordings, and it was a one-time study. They have not reported anything more on this.

Another set of evidence is the library of voices started by Leslie Flint made from the ectoplasm voice box.

There could be more work done researching electronic voice and computer recordings. Every little bit of evidence builds up a case. Thomas Edison was trying to build a machine to communicate with the dead, but he died before he got very far in its construction. When one of the great names in science and invention believed in the afterlife and wanted to research it, that says something.

In 1991, *Weekly World News* reported on a Soviet team led by Dr. P. Suslov, who trained thirty-seven dying patients in computer code and instructed them to communicate using the computer as a receiver once they were dead. The article cited one case, described only as Comrade K, who sent detailed messages about how great the afterlife was, saying that he was always near his family and couldn't wait for them to join him.

Trying to be thorough, I googled "Dr. Suslov afterlife." I couldn't find anything on him except the article from this paper, which was a supermarket rag; the lead story of the same paper was "Bigfoot Escapes – Kills Two." This was not the most credible research I have ever seen. The alien kidnapping story next to it was more believable.

The Scole Experiment

The best way to describe this series of experiments is complex and controversial. These sessions are supposed to have produced evidence of physical manifestations from a group of spirits, as well as proof of some mediumistic ability. Volumes of information have been written on this, and it has been hailed as everything from the greatest evidence for the presence of the spirit world to a hoax and everything in-between.

From 1993 to 1998, four mediums gathered in a cellar in the village of Scole in Norfolk, United Kingdom, to try to manifest spirits. After a year, things started happening, and they invited experts, including scientists, skeptics, and a magician. They also conducted an experiment in the United States, which was witnessed by numerous NASA scientists, who reportedly formed their own spirit group later. Three of the observers who were present at twelve sessions wrote a book, validating the occurrences.

Some skeptics have criticized the study harshly, and while they may make some good points, they leave out a lot of information about the study. That is always a red flag that suggests cherry-picking to debunk something. Here is a list of the manifestations in the study:

1. Lights darting all over the place – When the lights touched the observers, the observers felt pressure from them.
2. Voices coming out of mid-air
3. Tape recorders recording sounds and voices on playback
4. Spirits giving messages about how to build complicated instruments and recording devices. One

device, called a germanium box, was built and functioned better than a tape recorder.

5. Objects levitating
6. Disembodied hands appearing – Dr. Rupert Sheldrake, a reputable scientist with a great interest in the paranormal, reportedly gave one of these hands a handshake.
7. Orbs of light surrounding witnesses
8. A spirit giving personal information that was judged to be accurate
9. Complex images, messages, and even poems appearing on sealed film rolls.

This last manifestation is the most controversial. It is possible that the mediums switched the film rolls for pre-exposed rolls. One roll that was sealed against this potential tampering showed little evidence of imagery. In one case, an observer kept the roll in his possession and developed it immediately. There was mention of two faint star-like objects on that well-protected film. The striking images were from rolls in a locked wooden box, built to the specifications of the mediums. Some of these boxes are said to have had on them traces of acetate, which is used to put images on film.

The story is quite different depending on who reports it. According to skeptic sites there was nothing on the protected roll. They also claimed that most of the stunning images were already on the film in the lockbox, even though one witness claimed he had his hand on the box the whole time. There were spectacular things on the films: messages in many languages, symbols considered to be sacred and magical. Many people of good reputation are sure there was no tampering by the investigators. The usual argument against any afterlife connotations was that super-psi, similar to psychokinesis, was used to affect the film. If they had put the film in a lightproof container and turned on the lights, there would not be as much of a controversy around the film.

For my purposes, I don't think it helps me find what I want: proof that ordinary humans, not advanced high masters, are in the afterlife. The results of the Scole Experiment could suggest that there is a dimension populated by beings who were never of this world to begin with. Well, good for them. Maybe they punched their tickets to the afterlife as special creations long before humans showed up.

If the group running these seances could have gotten some recently dead run-of-the-mill humans to show up and give verifiable information about their lives that would require checking on sources not available to the participants, I would have been more enthusiastic.

It would be like if an angel showed up. All that would prove would be that there are higher beings. But what about people like us? Invite us to the party, and I would be a lot happier. Personally, I don't care if there are hundreds of angels dancing on the head of a pin; it has nothing to do with me and the rest of us surviving, unless one of these high-and-mighty beings could show me a long-form birth certificate to prove it was born as a human and then ascended. And it better not have materialized out of thin air – go down to city hall and bring me the original! I am probably just begging to get zapped by lightning for pissing off angels and ascended masters. I want to know about regular people in the afterlife. I don't know any of these high-and-mighty beings, so as proof of the afterlife for those I care about, this study does not exactly rock my world.

In an attempt to counter arguments that the cellar was rigged, with laser lights for instance, studies were held in six different countries. The results were less spectacular; however, some manifestations occurred.

These manifestations include a coin, jewellery, and flower petals raining down from the table to the floor and a newspaper appearing from 1944.

The experiments were concluded in 1998 and never repeated because the spirits warned that creating an opening between dimensions was affecting space-time.

It seems to me that if mediums are making contact between dimensions with the afterlife hundreds of thousands of times a day around the world, then space-time should be totally screwed. The spirits are said to come from a higher dimension, and one said he was a master, so maybe there is more of a penalty in opening higher dimensions to contact us than we thought.

There were a few problems with the Scole Experiment, however, including:

1. All the testing conditions were set by the mediums – the spirits wanted it that way.

2. In demonstrating physical manifestations, mediums are usually restrained and have their mouths taped, to prevent any trickery. The only restraints here were lighted wrist bands designed by the mediums. They didn't hold hands with observers, so the obvious argument made was that the mediums could get out of the bands, leaving them in place.

3. Sessions were held in darkness. Some observers said the darkness was not complete and there was a little bit of light, which might have come from all the luminous beings running around.

4. It is not clear if all doors were locked and all entrances sealed to prevent accomplices from entering and exiting in the dark. No metallic objects were allowed in the room. No night-vision goggles were permitted. I had no idea that spirits in high realms were afraid of metal, except when manifesting coins.

5. The question of film security has always been contentious.

6. The mediums, again according to the spirits' instructions, determined what recording equipment could be used. As soon as infrared cameras were suggested, the experiments were terminated.

I have avoided using this study as an example of the afterlife because it has nothing much to do with loved ones in an afterlife we can relate to, and the minor mediumship that goes on here involves contacting supposed entities not any deceased person. The spirits claimed to be in higher planes – one of them refers to himself as a master named Manu.

I'm fairly critical of the Scole Experiment because I think if the group had the power to call down spirits, then they should have called down a few people from the lower dimensions. Also, if they had done this, they could have done it in good light, since I'm sure they would not be as fussy as the masters about setting the conditions when such a powerful spirit group commands them.

The spirits in the lower dimension may not have been able to provide voices or create images on film, but I am sure they wouldn't have minded drawing a few pictures for us. It's true that they wouldn't be able to give important information to help advance mankind, but the only thing the Scole group did with the help of the higher spirits was build a fancy tape recorder, and humanity has not taken that and run with it to make the world a better place.

Reincarnation Studies

Dr. Ian Stevenson has been the primary investigator of cases where children claim to be someone else, especially in the Indian subcontinent. These children often give information it is very unlikely they would know, such as details about locations a fair distance away. When led to the town they talk about, they identify people and places accurately. These are supposed cases of reincarnation; the children were born within a few years of their death from a previous life and can point out these details in the same general area where that death occurred. In other cases, there are reports of children knowing different languages and having highly-developed musical skills that they say they learned in a previous lifetime.

I really do not know what to make of this. The most compelling case is of a boy about five years old who refused to eat milk curds because he said it killed him before. He said he had drowned after eating it. He then gave his name, and the name of his wife, described two stores he owned in a town that was several hours away. He was subsequently taken there and put through some tests, including repairing a piece of defective equipment in the soda biscuit factory the soul he incarnated with had owned. He correctly identified all his family members and knew the layout of the house. It turned out that the man had been eating far too many milk curds at a feast and died from internal damage in a bathtub. Dr. Stevenson was not involved until after the child visited the town, but he questioned everyone involved in detail and found out what happened.

Numerous similar cases, both in Asia and the United States, have been investigated by Dr. Stevenson. He was thorough in his assessments, and pronounced some cases unproven and others very likely to be true cases of reincarnation. Some critics have suggested that the children were coached by parents or overheard conversations and then imagined more. It is notable that all the memories of their past life are gone by age eight as their own persona develops.

Reincarnation would be evidence that a consciousness lives on for some time after death. The question in these cases is what happens as the child gets older? Does the dead person's soul leave the body somehow and go back to an afterlife or does it simply disintegrate? I am not a big fan of reincarnation. When I get to the afterlife, I want to stay there. It sounds a whole lot better than life on earth, and if my soul wants to grow and learn lessons by sending me back here to go through all this again, I am going to be uncooperative.

Indigenous People and the Spirit World

There have been reports of visits to the spirit world from many aboriginal tribes, including those in Australia, North America, and the Amazon basin. Most of these spiritual visits have been facilitated by medicine men or women and shamans, who are supposed to have gifts similar to mediums. It seems like these spiritual leaders can sense the spirit world, but they don't send their consciousness outside of their bodies. Some of these encounters with spirits happen after fasting, ritual drumming and dancing, and going on vision quests – long treks alone in harsh conditions. Other similar experiences require hallucinogenic drug use. If they sent their consciousness to the afterlife and conversed with spirits, that would be more proof that an afterlife exists, and getting to use drugs to get there is just a bonus. But that can't be documented to everyone's satisfaction.

I am adding these experiences here because they are almost lost memories of people who were conquered and nearly eradicated. Anthropologists are trying to retrieve as much information as possible, but the information about the spirit world from these tribes is a long way from being clarified.

There is a belief among some Native Americans that they live, or at least lived, halfway between this world and the spirit world. If we can find out the real story, we may find that people used to be able to have their consciousness leave the brain and survive to make these trips.

Aboriginal Australians tell similar stories, believing they split time between here and another place. This does not sound like the kind of information that proves the afterlife, and I don't know the details of any valid mediumship in that culture.

The next chapter about evidence given against the afterlife relies completely on the supposition that the entirety of personhood – every thought, action, emotion, personal characteristic, and memory – is only a product of brain activity. According to this supposition, nothing about a person exists outside the skull.

Aboriginal Australians, as previously mentioned, have been shown to know instantly when something has happened elsewhere. This means that information can exist outside of the mind. Although this example is not directly about the afterlife, if information from a human mind can be independent of the body, why can't it leave the body after death? If anything to do with conscious thoughts left the brain, they could measure it. No one has ever used equipment to measure a train of thought outside of the brain, and based on this, they conclude that no such thing exists.

I hardly think that I need to point out that, between dark matter and dark energy, scientists are unable to measure anything about 96 percent of all the constituents of the universe, so this seems like a rash statement to make about the lack of a soul because they can't measure it.

I will be the first to admit when evidence is weak, just as I am willing to point out when a medium is damaging the credibility of mediumship with their disregard for truth. I can afford to give ground because my argument can easily pull from a huge field of evidence. Skeptics can't afford to give an inch because they are on the edge of a crumbling cliff, by my estimation, as you will see in the next chapter.

SIX

Arguments Against the Afterlife

There are small groups of people obsessed with trying to prove that an afterlife does not exist. A group of authors got together to put many of the arguments against the afterlife into one book – *The Myth of an Afterlife: The Case against Life After Death*, edited by Keith Augustine and Michael Martin – to make it easier for someone looking for anti-afterlife material to access it. The group discusses the sparsity of evidence of an afterlife and the mountains of golden evidence that proves to them that to any rational person the afterlife does not exist. I am a rational person, and I know the afterlife exists, but then I have solid information from experiences that they have not had. They have my sympathy for that gap in their life experience, but they come on so strong, and they're so arrogant that I feel the need to respond. My response to them might seem harsh, but this is where the battlefield for hearts and minds on this issue must be fought, and I don't like losing to crusaders without a clue.

The Myth of an Afterlife (2015) was meant to be the encyclopedia for deniers of the afterlife: twenty-nine authors, thirty chapters, 675 pages. This tome was intended to redress the great injustice perpetrated on deniers by the book-buying public, who only gravitate to books supporting the "unwarranted" belief that there is an afterlife. Unfortunately for them, the book doesn't rank too high on the Amazon bestseller list (it sits at number 42,447 in Books). My theory on why their supporters aren't able to buy their books is the same reason the species known as the Loch Ness Monster can't purchase books: no money and poor credit ratings, or maybe, like that cryptozoologist's dream, there aren't enough of them.

This book was not warmly welcomed by a public starving for more material denying the afterlife. Is that because it is a bad book? No, it's because it's a *terrible* book, written by authors who use real neuroscientific findings, then overembellish them, add a bit of nonsense philosophy, and take multiple leaps of logic to conclude that they have shown overwhelming evidence that the afterlife does not exist.

It starts with a foreword by Steve Stewart-Williams, someone I've never heard of. This writer starts off arguing the conclusion of the book, by letting us know that the book provides all the evidence that is needed to deny the afterlife, and thus starts the discussion of the "evidence."

He laments that a meme throughout history all over the world has been a widespread belief in the afterlife. A meme is an idea that takes on a life of its own and is treated by everyone as obvious and correct, and Stewart-Williams sets out to destroy that meme right in front of our ignorant, irrational eyes.

The afterlife meme is attacked from the get-go with clumsy arguments. I'll describe his opinions on why all of us are irrational enough to believe in an afterlife. There are many opinions in this book that are just as poorly thought out as his, but I can't critique all thirty chapters, so I'll go into detail on this one, being as it's right up front.

First, he says we believe in the afterlife because of religion. This argument is faulty; people who do not belong to any organized religion believe in the existence of an afterlife.

Next, he says there is pressure to conform to the beliefs of society and pressure to maintain stability in a society of believers. How are these two separate arguments really different? In any case, the driving force holding religions and some nations together is hatred of other religions, not the belief in an afterlife.

Then he cites wishful thinking. This reason doesn't apply in my case. I would love if existence were just over and done with when I die. It is only my son's after-death communications that made me rethink that. I wouldn't want to go into a holding pattern, as glorious as it might be, if the cost is another trip back to this benighted planet.

Next, he mentions primitive science, where early man made up gods because they were scared of bad weather. This point is not only arrogant, but it's off topic. We don't know what people believed before writing was possible, and by the time we got the first afterlife beliefs from the Egyptians, they were sophisticated in sciences, architecture, and engineering. These civilizations were hardly primitive.

He then goes on to say the neuroscientific evidence will be so overwhelming that it will batter the afterlife believers into submission.

Keith Augustine, one of the editors, makes his first appearance in the Introduction. Augustine launches into a diatribe about how the neuroscientific evidence far outweighs the scant and flimsy evidence for the afterlife, with some more philosophical crap thrown in for good measure, to make it clear before any evidence is given that the afterlife belief is wrong. Augustine claims that the afterlife is possible, but says that the possibility is low and that when compared to the high probability of no afterlife, we must believe the high probability conclusion. We'll see how high that probability is by the time I'm done, compared with the high probability that I showed for the afterlife. This book discards my type of evidence as not worth even considering, claiming all of it is coming from delusional people. It then proceeds to describe their own data as a mountain of evidence, compared to the minuscule evidence for the afterlife. Numerous fallacious arguments follow when the rest of the authors throw their hats into the ring, and their contributions are represented as ironclad data.

After about five chapters of repeated information – the same data presented with slight twists – I saw where this was going. So instead of reading all of it, I looked at reviews online, and found overviews of and opinions on each chapter. Those reviews were NOT kind to the content of the book.

Just google the book and add "criticism." You can find where every chapter is harshly criticized for making too much of the science and for making conclusions the data did not support. I am going to touch on a few of the most pivotal arguments.

The overarching argument is that science has shown that every aspect of our consciousness is created by firing networks of neurons, and every part of consciousness can be mapped out. However, no one has been able to weigh, measure, or otherwise document the presence of anything more than this bunch of neural networks that have somehow achieved the ability to give us a unique personhood with thoughts, dreams, ambitions, a moral conscience, and the ability to make major changes in our outlook on life and its meaning when the situation warrants. There is no agreed-on definition of consciousness and absolutely no mechanism for how a group of cells can organize themselves to produce our consciousness, which makes each of us who we are. Notwithstanding that minor oversight, the author proceeds to explain how scientists have managed to limit all the various higher functions like thoughts to areas within the 1,400 or so grams of protoplasm that is the brain. They contend that nothing can leave the protection of these brain cells and carry information and awareness beyond the confines of the skull, so when the brain dies, all these higher non-physical elements of personality extinguish with it.

The evidence presented was gathered from subjects with brain damage or brain disease or subjects who have been given drugs or electrical stimulation to their brain. It was also pulled from imaging studies and a few oddball things like studying a railroad worker who got an iron bar jammed right through his left frontal cortex. One author kept harping on the fact that stimulating one neuron made the subject think of Halle Berry. One neuron! No one can isolate one neuron, and one neuron by itself cannot formulate a concept, so the so-called Halle Berry neuron is either an attempt to inject really lame humour into a dull book or it is just a false sensational claim.

Anti-afterlife activists constantly demand that afterlife research follow every aspect of scientific protocol, while they publish what are basically one-off studies, with no controls or double-blind protocol. I understand that you can't go around sticking iron bars in different parts of volunteers' heads to make for controls to help verify the evidence that a personality changed from sunny and cheerful to grumpy because the frontal lobe was damaged. This leads them to the conclusion that the frontal lobe is responsible for personality. I too would lose my charming personality and be pissed off for life if I got an iron bar jammed into any lobe in my head. This does not seem to be a great way to prove their theories.

They rely heavily on the fact that the personality is dependent on neurotransmitters, functioning in neural networks, by citing that antidepressants change the personality, thinking, and even impaired memory in people with anxiety, depression, bipolar disorder, and schizophrenia. The assertion that these medications, by way of mechanisms that they have worked out, cure mental illness is not nearly as strong as they try to have you believe.

This is where my experience in practising medicine comes in handy. Antidepressants do not work a lot of the time. Prozac, a drug that keeps more serotonin in the synapses between nerve cells, has been touted as the most effective antidepressant yet made because the research has shown that depression was caused by lack of serotonin activity. However, a new serotonin or serotonin-norepinephrine drug needs to be developed every few years, and since a lot of patients say the medications aren't helping them, we go to newer and newer medications, but they keep coming back with the same complaints. We even use medications designed for seizure disorders, and resort to electroconvulsive therapy in some cases, yet there is still an epidemic of mental illness out there. Some medications like bupropion and mirtazapine have no neurotransmitters identified as being associated with their actions. And there are no medications for personality disorders. Personality is a big part of consciousness research, and not one drug has been developed from this increasingly complete understanding of brain function and personality.

Medication cannot be used as proof that personality is limited to brain activity. They should not use this as evidence to support their argument that mental function and aspects of consciousness like moods reside in the mind. Their theory breaks down when applied to actual people. It's an ongoing mental health mess out there, and the authors of this book seem blithely unaware of it as they expend time and resources on trying to prove the afterlife does not exist.

These researchers are perfectly willing to pontificate on the great success of mental illness treatments to bolster their argument that the research pins down the exact parts and components of the brain that are responsible for moods and thoughts, saying the right drugs have been developed to work in the brain to relieve mental illness. Any doctor that has dealt with real patients can tell them that this important component of their argument – the primacy of brain tissue and its chemicals in determining who we really are and what we feel – is a total fallacy. The apparent mountain of evidence rapidly erodes when their major argument doesn't support that consciousness, a large part of which is mood, thoughts, and one's general personality, is as controllable as they allege.

They assume that correlation implies causation, when it is equally likely that the damaged area was the last link in a chain of causation for thoughts, words, and deeds. If I sprain an ankle, I can't run. Does that mean that the act of running was entirely controlled by my ankle?

The next line of evidence is that Alzheimer's disease patients lose function in identifiable areas of the brain, resulting in a significantly reduced ability to think, based on how these patients interact verbally and behaviourally with the world. It is true that in the elderly, there is usually a decrease in tissue in identifiable areas of the brain like the cortex, and often MRIs will show multiple areas that have been damaged by microinfarctions, where the blood flow to that part of the brain gets blocked. Most of those people, however, don't show any symptoms of dementia. Structure does not always correlate with function. These scientists manipulate structures, find that some cognitive functions are altered, and conclude that in that structure they have identified another building block of brain that is creating consciousness.

If you destroy the entire brain, you will not see that dead body demonstrating consciousness to you. That doesn't mean that the consciousness is extinguished forever. People are speaking to the conscious parts of the deceased all the time through mediums. Go ahead and document the complete destruction of a structure like the brain, and congratulate yourselves in having gotten rid of that pesky consciousness. I say pesky because that consciousness will let you know it is intact and functioning better than ever when it speaks to you through a medium.

The biggest part of dementia is memory loss, including the inability to remember who people are. There has not been any agreement on where memories are made and stored or evidence that specific memory areas are deteriorating. Another argument against this example of the brain structure and function being responsible for the symptoms of Alzheimer's is that some Alzheimer's patients have minutes of complete lucidity, especially when they are about to die. This phenomenon has been reported by hospital workers and families at the patient's bedside. Many of these reports involve the patient speaking as if deceased relatives or friends were present to accompany them to their new life after death. This is not widely reported, presumably because people are already being called liars for reporting patients temporarily regaining the ability to speak perfectly normally, becoming visibly more alert, and regaining memory.

With minds that are unable to imagine anything other than the physical things they sense with their five senses, the authors in *The Myth of an Afterlife* make ridiculous statements implying that if the consciousness of a patient with dementia sneaks by their detection equipment, it will always be demented. Mediums have talked to patients who have died with dementia, and they can hear them communicating without any impairment. It may take a while to get in touch with them, however, because it is said that someone who dies with dementia will need a longer time to get back their full faculties in the afterlife – however time is measured there.

There are many examples of people whose conscious mind functions, but they can't communicate that to anyone. For instance, a stroke can stop people from being able to speak, but when they regain function, they report they were thinking clearly and all their mental faculties were intact, but they just weren't able to communicate. Some people who have gone through this have kept notes on their experiences, but it is difficult to capture consciousness and deeper thoughts on paper.

The researchers' data presented in the book is built on invalid assumptions, and the book is full of examples showing that their information is not based on anything significant.

Instead of going through and debunking all of these examples, I'd like to look at one of the researchers they cite who often jumps to unwarranted conclusions. Dr. Susan Blackmore has spent a lot of energy denying that NDEs are examples of the consciousness leaving the body, and that instead they're caused by brain damage and hallucinations.

NDEs threaten the primary hypothesis of this group because their theory can't allow for the consciousness to leave the body and survive outside of the brain. This is the key argument required to state that the consciousness cannot survive brain death.

Dr. Blackmore is essentially their star witness if she can provide clear evidence that nothing separates from the body while patients in the millions say that their essence leaves and can look down on the body before going through the experiences that characterize NDEs, such as going through a tunnel. Dr. Blackmore makes an argument, denied by some qualified doctors, that hypoxia in the visual area of the brain is responsible for thinking one's disembodied consciousness is going through a tunnel of light. She repeatedly states that the drugs that affect neurotransmitters are responsible for hallucinating an out-of-body experience, or an NDE.

I don't know how many times it has to be pointed out to her that none of her drug experiments can simulate all aspects of NDEs.

She scrupulously avoids acknowledging the inconvenient fact that NDE patients can accurately report events and objects far away from their beds. For example, one patient correctly describes a tennis shoe on the hospital roof, including that the front of the shoe was scuffed. Did she sneak out of the bed I which she was being resuscitated while no one was looking, climb onto the roof, and return in ten seconds? Someone would have probably noticed a clinically dead woman scaling the hospital walls. This was a regular woman, not a superhero. If this is not proof that a hypersensitive consciousness left the body and travelled independent of the brain, how about a patient blind from birth reporting things seen in the NDE? Dr. Blackmore calls these lucky guesses.

There is incontrovertible evidence against NDEs being hallucinations, either due to trauma to a brain that has outwardly ceased functioning or brought on by using an array of drugs. There are more and more reports added to the record each day of something non-physical but fully aware – with heightened senses – travelling away from the body to observe distant events, which are later verified as accurate. How Dr. Blackmore casts doubts on and then flatly denies these reports in the face of solid evidence is beyond me. She has engaged with afterlife advocates, and she said if there was one documented case of remote seeing or a blind person describing things visually during an NDE, her conclusions would have to be reconsidered. She has been advised of several, and I have never seen her respond to this evidence.

Some have tried to rescue this sinking ship by suggesting they were using psychic powers like telepathy, clairvoyance, or super-ESP to know what was going on elsewhere, but these are all things that debunkers deny exist. Instead, they point to "The Amazing Randi's" fraudulent and rigged publicity stunt, known as the Million Dollar Challenge, where he would supposedly give one million dollars to anyone who demonstrates psychic powers.

But when they need to fix a broken foundation in their house of denial, psychic abilities magically appear! Honest science doesn't ignore data or come up with explanations the researchers previously said do not exist simply because that data invalidates their a priori conclusions on their current research. This is shooting yourself in the foot to save face.

Before agreeing that they are wrong and that the consciousness of a fully intact person, thoughts, memories, and all, can indeed survive outside the body, they want evidence. They suggest that experimental proof must be provided. Evidence of remote awareness is not enough for deniers. They demand certain kinds of evidence that someone's consciousness is detached from the body, such as playing cards placed where only a detached consciousness at ceiling level can see them and report which card was placed as part of an NDE. Cards have been placed in some hospital settings, and no such reports have been made.

Does this prove their point? There are several reasons I don't think it proves anything, and their intransigence on this is really irritating. A mind that leaves a body at the moment of death (or near death) to take a quick look at the body won't care about playing cards. Anyone who hangs around for any length of time is far more interested in what is going on with their resuscitation than in hunting down cards hidden on shelves.

The shortcomings of using playing cards as invalidation of NDEs should be easily apparent to anyone. When you leave your body, feel a great peace, and are drawn to a tunnel of light, it is unlikely that you are going to delay a trip to the afterlife to see if you can collect enough cards to get a good poker hand. Adding in the fact that most NDEs do not occur in a predictable location means stacking only ERs and ICUs with cards on the ceiling is a pointless exercise. NDEs happen in many places, such as around car accidents, near drownings, in ward beds, at home, and in nursing homes. Does it not make more sense to verify what a patient says they saw outside of the immediate location of the body that they are in the process of leaving than expecting them to search for playing cards, especially since they can't be told to search for the cards?

All the evidence of remote views already exists, from an accurate description of a woman noticing that a little girl in the waiting room was wearing mismatched clothes to people describing verified reports of the exact conditions at their homes at the time they reported being away from their bodies. Dr. Blackmore's argument that no consciousness leaves the body flies in the face of these verifiable reports, and it requires undisciplined thinking to publish it in a book or expound on it with James Randi standing next to you in one of his money-making debunking events and taking notes to go on YouTube and incite his rabble. At this point, the credibility of the deniers is being threatened beyond any hope of redemption.

As soon as there is evidence of one consciousness leaving a body and surviving outside the brain, twenty-nine authors can write whatever they want to try to deny that consciousness exists outside the body, but their arguments fail. All the philosophizing about karma, heaven and hell, iron rods in people's heads, and Halle Berry neurons becomes completely irrelevant.

The book argues that the soul is redundant since the brain can do everything. Another argument is that if the soul is inside a body, their instruments would detect it, since it must have mass and dimensions. What part of "non-physical" don't they understand? An argument is made that if the soul has no physical qualities, it cannot influence the body. Well, it does not have to influence the body if it's function is only to monitor the events in life. Spirits are composed of energy that cannot be detected and measured on this plane of existence. They are made up of a high vibration light, which appears to be able to come and go as necessary, carrying everything important encoded as light.

The physical evidence falls apart. There is no proven mechanism for how the neurons work together to produce personal consciousness, which is something greater than individual actions, individual thoughts, or the ability to describe sensations with stimulation.

The pioneer of brain stimulation, Dr. Wilder Penfield, started out to prove that the brain was indeed all that was needed for a fully functioning consciousness. After forty years of research, he concluded that something greater than brain tissue was needed to create consciousness. He suggested that the brain was like a computer that needed a programmer external – and superior – to it. Although that is just one man's opinion, it is an important contribution from a scientist who has done more work on this issue than any of the authors of this book.

There is at least as much philosophy as science in this book, and I am in no position to assess it. I have read great philosophical arguments about the afterlife on Ian Wardell's blog at ian-wardell.blogspot.ca and on the website Paranormalia at monkeywah.typepad.com. Keith Augustine has contributed to this site, but he felt he was being treated with hostility when arguments didn't go his way. He posted a response to all his many critics in another journal, but it didn't seem to change anyone's mind about the belief that his book reached an erroneous conclusion about the afterlife. This book, a compilation of all their arguments that apparently show the afterlife cannot exist, tries to mislead a public that doesn't know enough about the subject, and the weak arguments seem convincing because they are presented by contributors with some academic credentials.

In addition to presenting faulty arguments and evidence, *The Myth of an Afterlife* ignores data that would sink its scientific arguments. Rather than approaching the subject scientifically, the contributors have simply dismissed anything that disproves their predetermined conclusion as having no value. They spend a part of the book denigrating the verbal, sincere evidence given by millions of people as imaginary and useless. The least they could have done is acknowledge that anecdotal evidence and show by closely analyzing it what the flaws were in all this overwhelming data. It is data that would need to be refuted for them to prove their point.

This book is littered with straw men – false arguments they create that they can easily destroy.

Their argument that this brilliant work has shifted the burden of proof onto the people who believe in the survival of the persona is simply invalid. The more people with a grasp of real science or with a good background in philosophy who look at this book, the more the criticisms emerge.

Although these skeptics have nothing useful or valid to say, they say it in detail, and they keep repeating it incessantly, filling up 675 pages. They aren't converting anyone to their beliefs, and while there is an attempt by the debunker community to flood the internet with misinformation, the key to their effectiveness is whether they are making enough sense for anyone to consider buying into their unproven point of view.

While it is true that the existence or non-existence of the afterlife is not a matter of opinion polls, the fact that more people believe that the afterlife exists is a result of people weighing the evidence. Simply claiming that the evidence of extinction of the person after death far outweighs the evidence for post-mortem survival is not enough. That claim has to have some basis in reality, and the conclusion that many people have made after educated analysis is that it does not.

The one thing I can point out is that these pro-afterlife books outsell debunker books by probably ninety-nine to one. I don't believe it's just that book buyers prefer uplifting books. I believe it's mostly because debunkers really have no evidence; their books lack credibility and can only be of interest to their small core of fanatical followers.

People who pick these books up are likely turned off by their vitriolic, antagonistic, and argumentative tone. I'm not surprised that these books get published – they look good superficially. But very few people are buying the books, or their premise.

Anti-Afterlife Battles on YouTube – Giving Free Speech a Bad Name

I posted videos of Jordan on YouTube. I took a look around the site for intelligent information on the afterlife. I found TED talks by Fred Alan Wolf and Stuart Hameroff. I saw documentaries with "proof of life after death" in the title, but these were either NDE or religious videos. I also found far too many videos of Richard Dawkins expounding his views on the afterlife, based on being an atheist with no facts, just opinions.

Deniers

Many people online claim to have evidence that the afterlife doesn't exist. Quite a few of these people comment on issues far outside their field. I'll look at the arguments of one of the deniers I see most in videos, (other than James Randi, who does not present evidence, other than calling out everyone, and everything, he decides is a fraud, as a fraud), Dr. Sean Carroll.

Dr. Sean Carroll

Dr. Sean Carroll is now one of the leaders of the campaign against the afterlife. He claims there is strong evidence that the afterlife doesn't exist based on the fact that "All of the science of everyday life is fully understood," and the afterlife has been completely ruled out by this. His arguments are long and tedious, and he always seems to be debating opponents who do not challenge him directly on his statements.

His arguments come from different directions, but all seem to have two aims: to prove that the afterlife does not exist and to prove that God does not exist. According to Carroll, the universe was perfectly capable of producing itself without any external influence. In one video, he demonstrates how this was done by putting a dot on a chalkboard and saying this is the Big Bang, then draws lines to show parallel universes.

The no-God evidence was worse. Carroll describes a God and

rips it apart because the properties he ascribed to God were ridiculous – another case of building a straw man to destroy.

Carroll is a physicist who specializes in dark matter and dark energy, which constitutes around 96 percent of the universe. It's this part of the universe that all scientists have failed spectacularly to measure anything about, other than its gravitational effect, and gravity is the least understood of the forces in the universe. They know what it does, but not what it is. So now he dabbles in trying to show God and the afterlife do not exist.

His statement that the well-understood science regarding life rules out an afterlife just did not resonate with me. He takes it as a given that the brain is entirely responsible for consciousness and asserts that if there were something outside the brain interacting with the world, he would be able to measure it. The crux of the argument is that anything that can't be measured by scientists would be too weak to affect the matter in the brain. He ignores that there are forces in this world that are strong but still immeasurable. For instance, strong poltergeist activity has been documented, but no one has been able to measure it.

Carroll goes on to say that the brain is made of atoms and that we know everything there is to know about atoms. The first statement is true, but the second is up for debate. Carroll and others generate elementary particles in the Large Hadron Collider, but why do they keep looking if they know everything about subatomic particles already?

He says that when the brain dies, the atoms become much less active and go to their lowest energy state. He also says they disperse as the brain decomposes. Energy is released when any active system shuts down, and the key assumption Carroll makes is that this energy dissipates everywhere, losing its coherence and thus not retaining a personality.

Carroll believes in parallel universes and extra dimensions, which scientists will likely never be able to measure, yet he denies that an entity from a non-physical dimension exists because it cannot be measured using physical matter. How does anyone know what the unseen dimension is capable of? Because there is no way to know, all of Carroll's arguments based only on what we know about space-time don't apply when we are talking about something unseen, something that defies our ability to measure it, something with properties and powers we can't begin to imagine. Using the laws governing this universe, and finding that they fail to show anything about a plane of existence where these laws don't apply, doesn't constitute proof of its non-existence. So, it's true that our best efforts, using only the science available to us, do not show evidence of an afterlife. This is a far cry from Carroll's claim that the afterlife does not exist.

Sean Carroll is not the only one finding fame disputing the afterlife on shaky grounds. Michael Shermer, Sam Harris, Daniel Dennett, Richard Dawkins, and James Randi have a significant online presence and have written books saying there is no afterlife. None of them have evidence – they have a strong opinion and a desire to force it on others. No one should be intimidated to disagree with these well-known figures just because they have a strong media presence.

More Assessment of Evidence Presented against the Afterlife

Lawyer Victor Zammit has taken the leading scientists and magicians at their word. He uses statements they have repeated many times to complete a theoretical cross-examination of them. He shows that the spiritual realm is outside of the skeptics' knowledge base, and he argues that they have used their positions of trust and fame to make statements they are not qualified to make. The celebrity scientists that he has criticized include Stephen Hawking and Richard Dawkins. In each case, in violation of all scientific principles, they have refused to look at all the evidence. They have made claims about issues outside of their fields, which makes them basically laymen when it comes to the paranormal, as it is not directly related to anything they have achieved in their own work.

The gist of it is that they claim intellectual authority when they discuss the afterlife, and they don't have to look at and disprove available evidence before making definitive statements. Zammit, a paranormal researcher who has spent twenty-five years in this field, makes a good case that these people are in no better position to make statements than the afterlife researchers who have taken the time and effort to examine what the data have claimed about the afterlife, and concluded that it exists.

He further points out that these people use their position in academia to make statements that, as he puts it, are fraudulently spreading darkness around the world, and they're doing it to gain media exposure and to sell books. While I do not agree with everything on his website, this seems to be a valid point.

People who have lost loved ones and can't tell the difference between a truly learned opinion, and an opinion from a renowned scientist speaking on a topic in which their expertise is lacking, will be inclined to believe anything a famous scientist says, and believe falsely that their loved ones are gone forever, which can cause unnecessary pain.

The crowning touch to his accusations of fraudulent behaviour for financial gain, was his cross-examination of James Randi's statements. Dr. Zammit puts James Randi under the logical and legal microscope. Randi's constant response has always been that he does not need to look at evidence, as he is a qualified paranormal debunker, based on absolutely no credentials in that field. He has never looked at any data that derails his anti-afterlife crusade with the critical thinking that is supposed to be his strength. He simply says that psychics and mediums are all frauds, and keeps repeating it to stir up his fans. I have been in a long-running battle on YouTube posts with his fans who make the most sickening, fawning statements about this man who is some sort of demigod in their eyes, and I had written an entire chapter describing my interactions with them, but this part of the discussion about the erroneous evidence presented by deniers has gone on too long, so I've decided to cut out the online disagreements because I have already alluded to my defending mediumship to closed minds, and the viciousness that ensued.

I realize that when you have suffered a great loss, it is natural to wonder if there is a chance that your loved one still exists, and the natural inclination is to research whatever you can. But beware of YouTube – everyone around the world has the option of posting whatever they want. A pack mentality can develop, and people stop thinking and revert to viciously defending their territory.

In summary, the so-called evidence against the existence of the afterlife does not stand up to scrutiny. There is no substance there that should shake anyone's belief in an afterlife. This is a typical case of not accepting everything you hear or read as the truth, even if it comes from people that are admired by many. They too can be completely wrong, and in this case, I believe they are all dead wrong in saying that there is no such thing as an afterlife.

SEVEN

Scientific Theories on the Spirit and the Transition to the Afterlife

Serious thought has been given to explaining how a non-physical soul or spirit can be present in the body but successfully hide from skeptics, and how that entity can leave the body intact upon death, while avoiding detection by these same skeptics. I will describe some of the scientific theories to explain this phenomenon as best I can.

Many scientists who study this issue claim the burden is on afterlife believers to prove the afterlife exists.

For me, only when their science can explain how mediums know things that would otherwise be impossible for them to know can they say they proved anything.

The theories of scientists like Dr. Fred Alan Wolf and Dr. Stuart Hameroff have advanced our understanding of the possible science behind the afterlife. Other contributors include astronomer Dr. Bernard Haisch, Dr. Deepak Chopra, Dr. Ervin László, Dr. Pim van Lommel, and Maureen Vensclaar, who specializes in NDE research. I have not mentioned those doing experiments with mediums, or others on the extensive list of NDE researchers, as they deal with the data they collect, but do not necessarily address the physics of death and what is beyond.

There may be more theories that apply to the afterlife that I have not found, but I'll stick with the few here – there are enough to provide obstacles to those who claim that all science supports their denial of life after death.

Electron Theory

Dr. Fred Alan Wolf is a leader in quantum physics and a prolific author who has popularized advanced science by making it more accessible for laypeople. Dr. Wolf says that quantum physics necessitates dimensions outside of our own. He argues that electrons must go through a dimension we cannot detect when changing orbits. The term *quantum tunnelling* means that a particle disappears from here and comes back, suggesting there is a pathway from this universe into somewhere different and a pathway back.

An additional, but more complex, argument deals with how consciousness affects matter. I will try to simplify it. First, it's important to know electrons aren't little submicroscopic planet-like objects revolving around a sun-like nucleus, creating a little subatomic solar system. Each electron is a cloud of probability, and only when an observer looks does the electron assume a value of position and momentum. But what about all the other values implicit in the probability cloud? One school of thought suggests they immediately take on those values in other dimensions where an alternate version of the curious investigator is recording them. This doesn't explain the afterlife, but it shows that consciousness can affect matter and create dimensions. The suggestion that consciousness is the prime driver of the universe says that consciousness is not something created and confined by the brain. It does not rely on the brain and may exist after the body dies.

While this theory is not a theory of an individual afterlife per se, Dr. Wolf has provided a service to afterlife researchers by adding his name – and thus his reputation – to this field. He is just one of a long list of top-flight scientists, including several Nobel Prize winners, who have looked at the evidence and concluded that the afterlife exists. At the very least this provides a huge tipping of the scales toward those who are open-minded about the afterlife.

A Black Hole Theory

Maureen Venselaar has published her findings on the science of souls leaving the body in a book available only in Dutch, but she was kind enough to post a summary to the Near Death Experience Research Foundation website.

The Dutch seem to be very active in the field of NDEs and the afterlife. Dr. Pim van Lommel published an article in *The Lancet*, one of the most prestigious medical journals in the world, documenting forty-one cases of convincing NDEs. I mention that here because Dr. Venselaar focused her research on NDEs before branching out to other disciplines, such as astrophysics, cosmology, and biophysics. Her black hole theory has to do with speculations on actual death, not just NDEs.

As it was originally posted, the theory was simpler, which made parts of it look crazy, but Dr. Venselaar has published a more complete, technical explanation of the theory on connectedinthedeep.com that makes the theory seem more plausible.

She suggests that when a body has suffered serious trauma or illness, a reaction occurs at the subatomic level throughout the body. Photons, which are known to be discharged when electron orbits drop, are released in the shape of the body. They stay together while the body is alive and then leave when it dies, carrying all the information needed to create a body of light, with its memories and intact conscious personality, that will be recognizable to their loved ones who are already in the afterlife. No one has seen this body of light, which makes sense because it "vibrates" at such a high energy that we can't detect or measure it. I have heard of orbs of light appearing on film around dead bodies at funerals and elsewhere. They apparently even appear on cellphone cameras. These get dismissed as defects in the picture as no one has ever seen them in real time.

The photons Venselaar studies are biophotons, which have been measured by German researchers. There has been a report from Russia that suggests biophotons can transmit an infection from one bacteria to another some distance away. They concluded that photons could carry information across space to produce an infection, but could be blocked with UV resistant glass.

She reported that one physician, Dr. Chawla, measured huge surges of brain activity that lasted two to three minutes at the point of death. I checked the report. He apparently would not say this could be information leaving at death, but he suggested that the energy may play a role in NDEs. His finding suggests that a huge amount of energy is released just before death, and the length of time of this sustained energy release suggests that a lot of information can be uploaded to somewhere.

Biophotons are sent into the ultraviolet region of the electromagnetic spectrum, but no one has ever filmed this at death – it's impossible to do so in a hospital environment where far more powerful emissions from monitoring equipment and bright lights would drown out the biophotons (and you really shouldn't interfere with last ditch-efforts to save a life just to see if you can capture a glow on film).

These biophotons and the gigantic discharges from dying people suggest that light has somehow retained coherence enough to carry consciousness beyond the veil. Of course, the vibration of any discharged energy needs to increase by many orders of magnitude from that of blue light. The vibration rate in the afterlife is said to be far higher than anything on earth. Note that the word vibration used here is a bit different from the physical quality of vibration in science. It is just the closest word to approximate the quality in non-physical reality.

So far, so good. We have coherent light and energy leaving the body as it dies. All medical deficiencies are healed at this point.

This body heads for the standard tunnel of light. Venselaar suggests that it then becomes compressed to a size smaller than a grain of sand. In most NDEs people usually do not focus on what their bodies look like in the tunnel. Instead, they describe their consciousness moving at an unbelievable speed. She had described a light and a magnet, but amended that in the new article to point out that light and magnetism are part of the same thing. I think she's saying that we are travelling through a black hole toward a central light, and that the black hole is the tunnel, which is created by the compression of the light body.

She seems to be using the term black hole in a different way than physics describes black holes – a structure that draws in everything, and from which nothing can ever get back out. Describing this afterlife tunnel as a black hole seems to be a close enough analogy though. In it, colours are seen – initially as blue-green, which is how we see light coming toward something. The light appears red when it moves away – red-shift is a common term used to describe this.

Venselaar's theory would explain a lot and validate the fact that the consciousness leaves the body and travels away from it faster and faster. The more into the NDE a consciousness gets, the further away it gets from the body. This theory can also help explain how the person who has an NDE can accurately report distant objects. The light body can hang around for a bit and look about before it gets compressed and heads for the tunnel. This explanation destroys the deniers' assertion that nothing leaves the body after death, and it explains the remote seeing that many people have reported.

The biophoton body travels far faster than the speed of light, and time is always reported to be totally distorted in NDEs. It approaches a point where two universes meet at the end of the black hole. This would look like two cones meeting at their tips, with the light in between. The other side of the light is the entry point of the universe, which is the afterlife realm, where indestructible bodies of light exist. At this level of physics, you can't talk about times or distances – the afterlife realm isn't a faraway place; in fact, it likely exists all around us. As a long-term NDE researcher, Venselaar has information that beyond the welcoming light centre, the colours seen are pink-red. If you cross into that colour, you are moving away on the other side of the light and are dead to this universe, but your indestructible body of light will live on there and can contact us here.

As reported in NDEs, those who come back go to the very edge and can see and know the other universe. This is how people see dead relatives and report gaining all knowledge. Again, time doesn't matter here, so you can do a life review without it taking any length of time. The central light, described as a loving and caring realm with advanced caring beings or a being is also consistent with what is reported, with various NDE reports stating that it is God, Jesus, or other religious figures. This does not invalidate their experience, they are just using descriptions that they are culturally comfortable with to describe non-physical presences. Venselaar does not specify, but I assume that these are the higher beings that can cross over and back at will.

This is the point of decision. We only have accounts of people who decide to turn back and retreat through the black hole, re-expand the tiny grain of light into something the shape of the body, and re-enter, to be again restricted by the physical body, while remembering some details of information but losing all the infinite knowledge that they experienced at the point of decision because human brains have their limitations. People's brains are changed by NDEs, and it is widely reported that their whole outlook on life changes. A few even develop psychic abilities, maintaining a little bit of the ability to see completely into the other side, and they can become mediums.

There is science in this theory from a wide range of disciplines, but the scientists who are hardcore non-believers cannot accept it – they're stuck in thinking that is limited to this universe. This is why statements like "We know all about the physics of everyday life," cannot be used to rule out the afterlife. They simply aren't the truth. The true reality is above and beyond everyday life; otherwise we could not contact the other side – it's that universe that looks pink-red to the temporary visitor. Venselaar describes it as a warm, welcoming universe, where the laws of this universe obviously cannot apply.

I don't see anything apparently impossible with anything here. It is beyond our science, but nothing in science rules this out, as the debunkers believe. The only point that can be contested is referring to the tunnel as a black hole, since deniers will jump all over this, using properties postulated from the physics of this universe to flatly say that nothing can come back from a black hole. So, call it something else, the word *tunnel* is better, because it applies to the theory already stated by Dr. Wolf, where the term *quantum tunnelling* is used to describe what an electron does when it disappears from one energy level then reappears in another orbital level in the atom.

Some credibility for the afterlife theories come from different lines of research intersecting with each other. As I'm not a physicist, I am just reporting what I have read, and I'm analyzing it with what knowledge and skills I have. Any scientist with high specialization in one area can rip apart my logic, but my answer will always be "That's fine. I'm wrong on that point. Now explain to me how your science can explain the communications from Jordan that nothing in this universe that I know of can explain."

When I search online for up-to-date science dealing with these phenomena, I get the impression that new and vastly different theories are being proposed every few months, and find support from established scientists, and opposition from others. When we don't know about 96 percent of our own universe, how can anyone say anything is impossible?

Many have drifted into completely materialistic science (if we can't measure it, it doesn't exist), and reductionist science (if we can break it down to its smallest parts, we can know and explain anything). This would have been considered heresy by the founders of quantum physics, on which a lot of the world's technology depends. Max Planck has said many things warning against trusting scientists discarding consciousness. His ideas on this issue come down to his belief that all matter is derived from consciousness. He does make statements about a divine intelligence being behind all of it. This is guaranteed to bring derision from those who have made far lesser contributions to physics than Planck, but I don't think he was endorsing creationism or any specific religion; he is just saying that consciousness is universal and primary, which implies that the universe is intelligent. Consciousness is the battlefield on which the afterlife supporters and deniers meet, which is why the following theories have a lot of bearing on the science behind the afterlife.

Dr. Stuart Hameroff and Sir Roger Penrose – Orchestrated Objective Reduction (Orch-OR) Hypothesis

Hameroff, premier anesthesiologist, paired up with Penrose, a mathematical physicist, to study consciousness. They hypothesize that microtubules in the brain act as neuronal super quantum computers. Theirs is one of the best publicized theories of consciousness and the only one that has ever proposed what mechanism in the brain generates consciousness. It also says that this consciousness cannot be contained by the brain.

Microtubules are structures in neurons that were meant to only be structural components to keep the shape of the neuron intact. Hameroff and Penrose say that where the neurons can do 10^{15} computations at one time, the microtubules are actually quantum computers that can generate 10^{27} computations in that same time. They postulate that the microtubules have the property of superpositioning, being in two dimensions at the same time. Ignoring the antics of the deniers, who decided that consciousness resides only in brain tissue, these groundbreaking scientists clearly state their belief that computational ability in brain tissue of this magnitude has far too much power and cannot be confined to the brain.

Sir Roger Penrose says that his studies in space-time geometry suggest there is enough power to go outside space-time to a universal consciousness. The theory suggests that the microtubules' increased computing power allows them to send coherent energy outside of space and time into a universal consciousness. This theory does not make absolute statements about a personal consciousness existing forever, but it does say our conscious thoughts, feelings, and personality can leave our brain and join with something that has always been around and will be around for the foreseeable future.

Dr. Hameroff is more active than Penrose in explaining the theory of the universal consciousness, and each year seems more certain that it says that consciousness can survive without a living brain. He does not say that a unique personal consciousness is created, just that consciousness can flow from the brain and be part of a universal consciousness, but at least they have gotten conscious freed up from its dependence on brain tissue, another small step for science.

Contrast this nuanced attitude regarding some kind of preservation of our essence with that of the deniers, who continue to make absolute statements about consciousness disappearing when the brain dies.

Max Planck, whose work resulted in this computer I am using – and the better computer I want to get as this one is starting to really tick me off – would heartily agree that a universal consciousness is capable of existing outside of the confines of the brain.

Dr. Deepak Chopra supports this theory, and mathematical physicist Dr. Henry Stapp has similar theories. There are also the usual debunkers, but the theory has not gone away. This theory requires a universal consciousness for the microtubule quantum computer to interact with. Is there any suggestion that such a thing exists? For this, I turn to the theories of Dr. Ervin László.

Dr. Ervin László – The A-field

Dr. Ervin László is a science analyst. He has written numerous books on various subjects. The area of interest here is the Akasha field (A-field), a field that permeates all of creation and is conscious. The A-field is a quantum vacuum, a state in which you find the lowest possible energy. This field was first given a name thousands of years ago when Indian mystics were able to access a field of pure space with a complete oneness of the universe, and they termed it the Akasha. Dr. László drew on this knowledge, and shortened its name to the A-field. He has written widely on this, the most interesting of his books to me being *Science and the Reenchantment of the Cosmos* (2006).

He proposes properties for this field. The most scientifically supported concept is non-locality. In a nutshell, this means that information can travel instantaneously across the universe and everything in creation is connected to everything else. Information is not restricted to one location. This is what Einstein referred to as "spooky action at a distance," where two entangled particles can exchange information even if they are light years apart. Researchers have done experiments that have found particles exchanging information at 200 times the speed of light. This information must be travelling though the A-field, and equipment today has limitations, so it is not likely to be able measure infinite speeds.

This field, referred to as pure undifferentiated light, was the first thing created. It is the suggested cause of the Big Bang. We know it transmits things quickly, but is it conscious?

The A-field also supposedly records everything that has ever happened in creation. While that concept of the A-field is unproven, there are aspects of our universe that suggest a lot of information exists in some sphere.

Many people believe intelligence had to be involved to create such a fine-tuned universe. To maintain a universe with suns, planets, and life, at least six properties of matter and space-time can't be off by even a minuscule percentage. Examples include the strength of gravity and the properties of the weak and strong nuclear forces.

The theory that a field, which has been around forever, records everything, analyzes it like a computer, and comes up with the right answer to create a universe makes sense to me.

After what I have witnessed with mediums, the theory of multiple parallel universes many physicists believe in is no more likely than mediums speaking to the deceased, and these are not mutually exclusive.

I believe Dr. László's idea that the property of the A-field, having a record of all the universes – failed or functional – is the best way of explaining the inherit order allowing the existence of our life-friendly universe. Any field that uses the record of the failures and successes to optimize each new universe it creates, sounds like an entity that engages in thinking, analysis, and planning – all the ingredients of consciousness. And so, this universal consciousness allows for the Orch-OR theory to have a basis. These scientific theories are starting to come together in a meaningful way.

As soon as universal consciousness comes into play, the theory that the brain is the sole creator of consciousness is in trouble. Anti-afterlife scientists have sought to explain the mechanism by which brain cells produce consciousness without success; instead of proving it, they have taken it as a given. They propose the concept of a bottom-up mechanism of consciousness: the brain creates it. Although there is no evidence for it, this tenet allows them to dismantle afterlife theories.

The alternative explanation of consciousness is that the brain is merely a receiver of instructions from a higher consciousness, in the same way a TV receives broadcasted waves. You can tinker with parts of a TV and affect the picture, but the signal coming at it is not affected. You can tinker with a brain and affect how the body reacts, but the guiding consciousness is unaffected. This is the top-down theory of consciousness that says consciousness does not need the brain; the brain is just a receiver, and therefore it can die without affecting the consciousness. Consciousness lives on, like the TV signal, if someone destroys the set. We can't see the TV signals, and we can't measure what exists in the non-physical reality, yet both can have an influence on things in this world.

There is no more proof that the brain is the sole source of consciousness than there is for it just being a transceiver, used to carry out the will of the universal consciousness. Neuroscientists can tinker with the receiver (the brain) all they want and learn no more about the broadcast signal (consciousness) than someone would get by taking apart a TV set to understand the TV signals all around.

Science is nibbling at the edges of learning about this universal field, which underpins and interacts with all of creation. The demonstration of non-locality, by measuring the incredible speed at which information between entangled particles is exchanged is the best example. The key to the physics of the soul may be somewhere in this and other quantum theories.

Dr. Bernard Haisch – The God Theory

Dr. Bernard Haisch is an astronomer and cosmologist with some formal religious training, but he does not allow any specific religion to influence his theory. He has cooperated with brilliant physicists and mathematicians in his work on the quantum vacuum.

He sees the quantum vacuum as others have seen it – as an infinite, powerful realm of energy. He says that light and power are created by a creator, and when the universe was created, it would have been pointless for it to be like the undifferentiated infinite power of the quantum vacuum. The formation of matter requires a filter, so we can get contrasts. Through this reduction from the all-powerful to the material, we get individuality and differences, similar to how a movie theatre projector filters the plain white light through film to produce individual elements that show up on the screen.

Haisch makes three points:

1. The universe is here.
2. The universe was created.
3. There must be a creator.

This all-powerful creator wanted to experience itself, and to experience material life, it reduced its infinite nature by forming its creations, producing other simpler forms of itself.

Haisch suggests, based on the presence of the spiritual plane, that this creative force placed trillions of pieces of its infinite self in this spiritual plane until the process it set in motion could receive them as a soul. Since God (the creator) is in every atom of creation, everything has a piece of God in it. Everything sprang from the source, and every living thing has as complex a soul, or piece of God, as its size and complexity allow.

One of the arguments in *The Myth of an Afterlife* is that evolutionary development is a good argument against the soul, since it seems unlikely that it would suddenly pop into being in humans, as there was a gradual development from single-celled organisms to humankind. If we assume bacteria do not have souls, where in the evolutionary chain does a soul develop? There would have been two parents without a soul giving birth to an offspring with a soul somewhere along the line for us to have a soul. This concept answers that question.

Although there is no proof for this, something like this must have happened for there to be a spiritual plane for us to contact, and millions of us have done so. I have no idea at what point God started incarnating special souls (the stored pieces directly from its own self, fashioned at the dawn of creation) into humans, and then receiving them back on the spirit plane when their existence on earth ended.

The crucial concept here is that the soul is God, and God cannot die; therefore, the soul cannot die. God would be killing himself if that happened.

The Etheric Body Theory

The etheric body theory, put forward by Charles Webster Leadbeater and Annie Besant, though not very scientific, explains how a spirit makes the transition from a dying body.

Their main claim is that we have four bodies. The first two are the physical body and the propagating body – in other words, a living body. At death, both of these are toast. Then there is the astral body and the etheric body. These exist within but also beyond the physical body (and they can kind of stick out of them), which explains why people often see a halo or an aura around a physical body. Kirlian photography, which is a type of contact photography that uses electricity to expose the image, has captured this energy field around many living things.

The astral body exists outside of the body and can go on excursions or do what's called astral travel. (I would love to go to the astral plane and get hold of the Akashic records, so I could erase some stuff about me.) At the point of death, the astral and etheric bodies slide out of the body and head for the tunnel – and there's no messy science involved.

So, we don't have testable theories at the moment using science to provide evidence of the afterlife. But some high-powered people are beginning to lead the way, and I could list pages of names of respected scientists who believe in an afterlife or who are pursuing studies into this. But that seems like pointless overkill, and while many of them are leaders in their fields, most people would not recognize the names.

EIGHT

Descriptions of the Afterlife

I got so caught up in my medium sessions that I kept forgetting to ask Jordan what the afterlife was really like. Tony says he can tell me a bit: he remembers zooming around the universe by thought, and he said time doesn't pass the same way it does here.

Many people who are interested in the afterlife share their knowledge of it online. A lot of these accounts are so similarly – and obviously – wrong that you would think all the storytellers had read the same book full of contradictions. And of course, religions have contradicting conceptions of the afterlife, and none of them seem to match the picture most mediums paint of it.

Because of all these contradictions, I decided extensive research was needed to separate the wheat from the chaff (in the end, I found there was little wheat left).

The confusion around this subject was extensive. But I promised I would write a book to help people wanting to know about the afterlife, where their loved ones are, and where we are all going, so I sifted through the information.

I read book after book, then I looked online at Wikipedia and afterlife websites.

Wikipedia had the afterlife beliefs of many religions. I'll summarize these into categories of common beliefs.

Some religions believe in eternal damnation. From what I understand of the rules, you only have one lifetime and one chance to get it right. You can avoid damnation only if you read your scripture or loudly praise your deity regularly, and you're not off the hook even if you die as an infant, have mental illness, or were born into a society where you would be brutally killed if you refused to kill everyone outside of your religion.

Then, there are some religions that believe you go through trials and tribulations after you die, and you return to earth when you're done. Many religions that believe in reincarnation think karma can make you come back in different forms depending on how you acted in your previous life.

Then, there are the beliefs that your soul lies in the grave until the last day when you will be judged and get your ticket to your eternal destination. Some say that if you were good, you lie at peace, and if you were bad, you writhe in torment in the grave. How unbearable is that tension?

Zoroastrians also take the guesswork out of what happens in the afterlife. They believe after you die, you stay three days on earth with your spirit sitting up in bed with a pretty woman or crying at the foot of the bed with an ugly hag for company. When you have to be judged, you walk across a wide bridge, which narrows down to a blade edge, and if your sins weigh you down, you fall off, and are dragged down to damnation.

There are only two religious concepts in line with my beliefs. First, the Bahá'í faith says we immediately go to a good afterlife between incarnations but we can never know what it's like. I agree with the first part, but I believe we can know what it's like. To understand the afterlife, I defer to the Wiccan belief that spirits go to The Summerland, which is a place of reflection.

My son, his mom, and all of my family and friends are in this place of reflection. Other than spirits who were completely evil when they lived, everyone gets there eventually. It has been also said that even the evil can eventually make the decision to come into the light, but, as with everyone, will have to experience the pain they caused, before rehabilitation. I find peace knowing that everyone I care about will end up in The Summerland.

I still wanted more details about the fate of the spirit, especially those within the belief systems I incline toward based on information I have gotten from mediums or read in books by mediums. Some call this belief system Spiritism, which I am not entirely thrilled about, as it has connotations of seances and dark rooms, tables hopping about, and ectoplasm everywhere. There were many differing opinions given about these planes, so I had to try to come up with a consensus. I looked at what the opinions had in common, and got an approximation of what things are like once you cross over.

First, there is the earth plane. Some spirits are so attached to this plane that they can linger here for hundreds of years. Examples of these spirits include ghosts, spectres, and jinn.

Most people agree the next plane is the closest one to earth, but descriptions of it differ widely. I gathered information from theafterlife.com to try to put a picture together. I recognize this site isn't an infallible source, but it has an eclectic array of opinions from various people, including Edgar Cayce, Sylvia Browne, and Emanuel Swedenborg. (Swedenborg was accomplished in many areas of life, but people stopped listening when he described talking to the inhabitants of every planet in the solar system.)

The lowest afterlife level is controversial. Claims are made that it is like earth, but much worse, where everyone harms everyone else. This is the apparent source of demon possession. The demon possession is interesting. One scaremonger suggested that if you use drugs heavily and leave your body, a demon takes the opportunity to possess you immediately. The dissemination of this knowledge would make a better anti-drug campaign than the "say no to drugs" effort.

Most people believe that this level is called the lower astral plane. Others say it is just like earth, but drab (what earth itself is for most people). In any case, avoid this one and try for The Summerland.

If you fall short, aim for the higher astral plane, which is exactly like earth but a bit nicer, with a finer material making up everything.

All the descriptions of these two levels are hard to reconcile with the idea of the afterlife being outside of time and space. It can't be just like earth when time is not supposed to be like it is here and space as we know it does not exist. At best, these are the waiting rooms for the real afterlife.

The third level of the afterlife is by far the most popular, unless you want to venture into the levels of ascended masters, saints, and the like. Those who pontificate on the third level in so much detail have made their information a ready target for ridicule. There is a lot of foolishness out there, and it's hard to get good information on the higher levels, but I may as well cover the highest levels and get that out of the way.

Depending on who you read, there is anywhere from four to seven levels of the afterlife (and at least one version with eleven levels). The ultimate level is always a return to the Void – i.e., becoming one with God. At this level, no individuality is allowed, and thus I don't understand why anyone would want to return to the Void.

Above level three, the next two levels are thought and causation, where the brightest minds from earth are continuing to do experiments and sending the inspirations back to earth. We do not usually get much contact from here. Unlike the other mediums that only speak to the third level, Susan Lander reports in *Conversations with History* that she has many luminaries meet with her in her kitchen to tell her about the wonderful research they are doing and sending back to the physical plane. (I really wish they would stop wasting time in this woman's kitchen, and get back to work.)

The couple of levels above are coming closer and closer to the Godhead. More than one person has said these celestial levels are what masters like Jesus and Buddha aspire to. This contradicts what Christians believe about Jesus, i.e. that he is part of the triune Godhead and already so far past these levels he can't see them. It also contradicts the Buddhists' belief that the Buddha attained Nirvana and has already absorbed into God himself, and therefore has relinquished his individuality.

The rest of the levels move toward becoming pure thought. The final levels involve becoming one with God.

My interest lies in the afterlife rather than the return to God, so I want to get a handle on level three.

There are disagreements about the actual layout of the place. Sylvia Browne has published pictures of the buildings that exist there.

Browne says the makeup of this level consists of the following buildings:

> 1. The Hall of Learning – This is a huge library, with classrooms, where spirits learn and advance. This

topic is hotly disputed by the expert spirit consulted by the writers on Afterlife 101, who says there is no such building.

2. The Towers – Confused spirits are first sent here when they arrive.
3. The Hall of Records – This is where you find out who's been naughty or nice.
4. The Scanning Room – This looks like a control room in Atlantis, where the panoramic life review occurs.

Most people don't believe Browne's representation of the afterlife. She has described the afterlife as a replica earth with structures like the Pyramids and the Great Wall of China. She also said that Atlantis and Lemuria were in their respective oceans.

The ectoplasmic-voice-box people were also vitally interested in the landscape of the afterlife. They got full descriptions, the most detailed of which was from a woman who sold flowers outside a railway station in London before dying. She lives in a nice cottage in afterlife England. She likes tea and can cause a pot of it to materialize using her thoughts. There was no explanation of how a body of light drinks cup after cup of tea and no details provided on how she peed.

The spirits the voice-box folks talked to said there are flowers in the afterlife, but that you can't pick them because that would be considered killing. Oscar Wilde's spirit came through and said he lived in the nearest thing to a town, where he could go see plays by Shakespeare, who was doing his greatest work, or a concert by afterlife Mozart. This didn't really interest me because I'm not much into Shakespeare or Mozart, but if Elvis and Michael Jackson were taking their work up a notch, I'd probably check it out.

Others have made their unique contributions, with gems like the following: at one level we graduate from bodies of light to bodies of flame, so we can visit suns and not get burned.

There are no bugs in the afterlife. I thought we were all God's creatures, but I guess bugs don't make the cut. The grass is greener, the colours are brighter, and birds' feathers are nicer. The temperature is always a perfect 70 degrees Fahrenheit. The afterlife has been spared the metric system, I guess.

When it comes to the afterlife, many others appear to be playing fast and loose with some unusual ideas.

In *Afterlife: Uncovering the Secrets of Life after Death*, Barry Eaton says when terrorists show up they just sit around a fire in a circle ignoring everyone else.

Annie Kagan's *The Afterlife of Billy Fingers* features an express trip through all the levels to a union with God within a couple of years in earth time.

A lot of people agree, and it makes sense to me, that the afterlife shares the same space with us but at a higher vibration that only mediums can reach. However, Browne added a vexing detail that the afterlife exists three feet above ground level.

Others have made the following (fairly ridiculous) claims:

1. Spirits can talk on regular phones, and they can send us text messages.

2. Spirits can cause pennies with the sender or recipient's birth year on them to rain down from the ceiling.

3. Spirits can ring doorbells, but when you answer, there's no one there.

4. If you are not attractive, you will be attractive in the afterlife because of the light shining from your face.

Every description of the afterlife has been counteracted by another person's "authoritative source." I'm skeptical of these descriptions that sell books, but not skeptical that there is an afterlife. So many of the sites that claim they are an authority on the afterlife are riddled with advertisements for paid readings from a medium. They also often feature stores where you can buy this valuable information in book form, or buy T-shirts with psychic symbols, crystals, or beads that cost five dollars to make for a bargain price of just over a hundred dollars. These sites are only fuelling the debunkers' arguments.

I think we ought to do a reality check. I understand some science that may apply.

1. We know there is an afterlife.
2. The afterlife is not in this universe.
3. Light is paramount in the afterlife. Time, as we know it, does not exist for light; it only exists for our observation of light. So, light bodies theoretically should be massless and travel between realms instantaneously.
4. In that kind of time frame, it is possible that all events are stacked up, rather than being arranged linearly, and you can just pull one event out of the stack and experience it.
5. As for space, we do not know the first thing about the dimensional properties of anything resembling space in non-physical reality. Nikola Tesla has been quoted as saying, "The day science begins to study non-physical phenomena, it will make more progress in one decade than in all the previous centuries of its existence." Unfortunately, it will be a long time before we're able to make this progress since there is no funding available for the study of non-physical phenomena. The current direction that physics has taken has been going on for about eighty years. There is far too much invested in equipment, attitudes, careers, and scientists' reputations as leaders in their fields if these fields become obsolete.

But what about the outside of our space issue? Even the scientists who deny the afterlife buy into quantum mechanics and the string theory, and these theories demand the existence of other dimensions.

The truth is that no one knows what the afterlife is truly like, but it sounds like a nice place to hang out for hundreds of years, kicking back and having fun with family and friends.

And so it seems to me there's no need to fear death; the real struggle is life.

PART 3

Continuing the Search

NINE

A Plan for Finding Out Missing Afterlife Information

While I have received validating information that the afterlife exists and that my son is communicating in real time from there, I realize there are people who need to believe that the deceased still exist, but who have not had real evidence and may be considering seeing a medium or are interested in learning about the mechanics of the soul. My search for evidence of how the soul works has been fairly extensive, especially looking at how science can explain it. While I may have missed some legitimate information on the topic, I did the best I could.

I have come up with another way to answer these important questions. I cannot do it myself; it requires a group of mediums working together on the issue. They should do this for their own benefit because mediumship is being attacked relentlessly in public forums, and that ongoing and increasing criticism could hurt their careers. Mediums have a vested interest in silencing critics, or at least in gathering more believers by participating in this exercise to find answers to four questions:

1. Exactly how and when does a soul incarnate into a body?

2. What does the soul actually do during a person's life, and where is it?

3. What processes allow the soul to leave the body at death, carrying the persona of the deceased to the afterlife?

4. How does the person "live" in the afterlife outside of time and space and what exactly is the afterlife like?

I have written up what I could find out, but there are only theories around, and actual information giving details of the soul and the afterlife is extremely suspect, if not flat-out wrong. That is not to say that they don't exist. I know they do.

I have one idea about how to deal with all this uncertainty, and get much clearer answers, that may eventually help science to show that the existence of the afterlife and the soul, is extremely probable, and with a high degree of certainty.

Here is the plan in detail:

1. Mediums that have influence and public attention need to devote much more time to doing private readings, and in that time, spend a couple of minutes asking the spirit if they would give an answer to just one of the questions I have listed above.

2. Public mediums should then establish a collaboration with other good mediums who are not public figures and ask them to do the same: ask one of the questions above.

3. Establish a web page where mediums can post answers to these specific questions. Of course, they would need to make sure that all four are more or less equally covered. As the answers build up, we should be able to see similarities.

4. There are organizations of scientists, like Dr. Dean Radin's group for paranormal studies, who can rigorously analyze this growing collection of specific data and get far more detailed information about these issues.

These steps should not be too burdensome – the medium is asking for only two minutes of the deceased's time, a website is not expensive, and analysis of data is done regularly within many organizations.

If this book reaches enough people to give me credibility, I will make the calls myself, and learn how to set up a website, or ask an established institute to coordinate this effort.

This project (which I would call "The Human Soul Project") requires the mediums' willingness to participate, and with just a small effort, they could advance the cause of mediumship a long way and provide an unassailable foundation for their work. This will help everyone. It will go a long way to discredit the skeptics in the eyes of the public.

TEN

Jordan's Legacy – Proving the Afterlife

My son is dead to this world, and because of that I will never be the same. I swore on his coffin that I will never be happy in this world again. I miss his living presence here, where I can be with him every day. I have given up a lot as part of my mourning, including my career in medicine, a difficult but necessary action. I have gained the trust and love of hundreds of patients who have helped support me through my loss. I know I will never be the same doctor I was. My mind is too distracted. The worsening depression that comes from a real and tragic loss causes my focus to waver and my ability to care about every aspect of my patient's lives to wander.

Depression has caused me to lose motivation and interest in the world. It has altered my internal world, making me feel at odds with other people. It feels like no one understands how my mind works. Every task is challenging; dealing with things like taxes, finances, government regulations, and deadlines just makes me want to lash out at the demands and uncaring attitudes of bureaucrats. In fact, I want to lash out at everyone. Formerly important things matter very little to me. I go out as little as possible. I have a difficult time dealing with people who are enjoying their lives. Special occasions like Christmas are especially difficult. The warm feelings that this special time once generated are now a thing of the past, and I know I will never be able to feel them again.

Deep down, I know not to judge when people have fun as if nothing tragic happened. Their minds are not forever in the dark place mine is in and will be as long as my heart beats and I still breathe. It is not a matter of choice on my part to live a shadow life, putting in time until I can be with my son, Jordan, and all my family and friends who have made the epic journey from earth to our real, eternal home. It is all I am capable of, weighed down by a sorrow, and sometimes horror, when I contemplate the reality: I saw my twenty-two-year-old son, with his whole life ahead of him, stiff, cold and unbelievably dead. That vision will never lift.

Because my son has made that journey and has come out at a good destination, I have no fear of the episode called death. At this point, I no longer care if it is quick and painless or prolonged and painful. I know if I have a fatal illness, I will not try to hang on to this world for as long as I can. I will go back home with no complaints. I will not "rage against the dying of the light" – the light is dim, and most of the time I am in darkness.

But I'm still not at peace giving up. I still have my daughter, Alannah, to look after. She is living with me again, and there are times she really needs my help. I love her too. She is mostly independent at twenty-three years old, but there are times when she is ill or feeling down and needs her dad around. She suffers like me, but she has trouble dealing with the medical system and sometimes needs my help with that. I can't stand to see her in any kind of pain. Because of her, I will live out my natural life, but I am not fighting as hard as most people to stay here. I don't take care of my health. Everything in life, other than my family and friends and the empathy I feel for people who have gone through what I did, is no longer important.

My situation is not completely hopeless. I would not be here if it was. A little light of love and hope persists, and a little bit of life and purpose lie ahead of me. I did not know or care about a life contemplating purpose, spirit, dying, death, or the afterlife before Jordan gave up his life. Every death supposedly has a purpose. I do not claim to know entirely what the purpose of Jordan's death was, but I do know that it awakened something in me that is of value. It is something that powers greater than me tried to do on July 11, 1991, but I was not open to the spirit at that time.

That day, I walked away alive from a horrendous car accident. The Corvette was completely wrecked on the highway. Every part of the car was smashed in, except for where I was sitting, and it was on fire. When I got out, all that was there was a scratch on the inside of each wrist and a scratch on the top of my right foot. During the accident, I felt a protective layer of something like gel covering me.

No one could believe what had happened. People said it was a million-to-one chance that anyone could survive what I had. When I talked to the police officer that day, I remember saying to him, "Your left wrist hurts. I can fix that." I touched his left wrist briefly and felt some kind of current pass through my hand to his.

That was basically the end of the episode for that day. They drove me back to my parents' house where I was staying, and I don't remember much else. I had no alcohol or drugs in my system other than several prescribed antidepressants. I wrote it off as a lucky break. The odds of my surviving that accident were incredibly low.

Strange things kept happening over the next few days. At an Alcoholics Anonymous meeting, I could see a glowing light in the people around me, and I felt the warmth of their caring. Something was clearly off, and I was admitted to the hospital two days later. The doctors who saw me believed my visions were a result of the combination of my medication, my prolonged history of drug and alcohol abuse, and some underlying mental illness. My medications were changed, and I was released.

The police officer I had spoken to after the crash came over two weeks later and said he had written up a lot of tickets that would have amounted to hundreds of dollars, but he tore them all up because his wrist that had hurt and affected his whole life for ten years was pain-free and fully functional since I had touched it.

Ignoring a Spiritual Sign – In Retrospect

Because of the injuries to my wrists and foot, some friends and family members suggested these were holy stigmata, and tried to tell me I was saved by Jesus.

I could not explain why I had been protected or given temporary healing ability, but I was an agnostic at the time, so I ignored the entire thing. Looking back, I now think the episode was likely a sign to change, to look inside to find my spiritual self, change the course of my life – to do something different, something better.

These unusual events did not have much effect on me. I rationalized everything. Only now it seems fated, as a demonstration, as something had seemed to compel me to get out of bed at 5:30 am and drive for no reason. It felt as though I was being carefully directed, as though something wanted me to have that experience in order to change my life path.

I mention this experience because Jordan had to die before I would change, which is far too high a price for him to pay. I didn't listen at the time; it took Jordan's death to force me to look deep inside myself for life's answers regarding purpose.

I am sure that I was not capable of fulfilling any useful purpose by changing my life's path at that time – the call came at the wrong time for me. If I had changed the trajectory of my life, Jordan would never have been born; he would never have lived for twenty-two years; he would never have touched the lives of so many people.

I will not let his sacrifice be in vain. I will do what I failed to do in 1991: work with the spirit. Jordan is a spirit now, and I need to do what I must do to honour him always.

I was persuaded to write this book, but I resisted. I don't think I have ever seen life as other people have; things came too easily for me, and I was never grateful. I threw away many talents and gifts I was born with and lived life as an alcoholic and a drug addict, as well as a workaholic. I was never an authentic person. I was never a human being; I was a human doing.

Other people in my life have paid a heavy price for my failings, but the greatest price paid was something of untold value, the life of my beloved Jordan. I can never be worthy of such a price, but I now must do the best I can and try to contribute something useful as a lasting tribute to him.

I have recognized the great gift that Jordan has given me, the immense treasure of knowing that there is far more to reality than my blinders had let me see previously. He died and immediately started communicating in a way that unmistakably proved the afterlife. There can be no doubt about this. His communications have been specific and unique. No one on earth could have gotten the information they gave me. It is unmistakably from Jordan. When I falter and go into a prolonged deep depression, my friends and family tell me that this is not how Jordan would want me to live. He has said the same to mediums. I still struggle with this desire of his. I'm not sure why.

He lives in another place and now I have every assurance of joining him there. Since Jordan lives, and others have proven that they too live, we will all live when the bodies we inhabit die. We are currently earthbound, and when we lose a loved one from this place, we are devastated because everything in this existence has changed.

We are all here for a purpose, and it is not up to anyone of us to judge another soul's purpose in this lifetime, regardless of how good or bad their actions are.

We are here with imperfect knowledge and completely forget who we really are. Some of us have suffered great loss and the grief that goes with it, but many of us suffering have been given a great gift. We now have the absolute knowledge that we have a greater home and a true life awaiting us when we are finished doing what we came here to do. Some people's life purpose seems to be to hide this truth from us, and to lead us into dark places. I can now see that I shouldn't get angry about the harm they are causing, but I have to accept that reality is what it is and that only the creator knows why all this is happening.

I don't have to allow the harmful actions of others to go unchecked. In fact, writing a book that puts to rest the doubts about a good afterlife, which deniers keep putting forward, may be my final purpose. I will find out when this is over, and I go back home. In the meantime, I will continue to look for more and more evidence of the afterlife.

I will keep up with new research to conclusively prove that we are in contact with the dead in an afterlife. But I am not planning on writing any follow-up books on this topic. I won't open my heart to the world like this again – this was already too much.

As far as the afterlife is concerned, it is a done deal for me. I always trusted Jordan in life, and I trust him even more in death. We have enough proof of an afterlife, and we can all look forward to it as long as we do what we came back to earth to do.

I hope I have given plenty of reasons in this book to believe that the afterlife is real. I feel that I have been guided through this by others that know more than I do on the topic. In some parts of this book, I have shared incredibly personal information. I promise I am reporting these remarkable occurrences truthfully. I really have nothing to gain by misleading people because that would mean I was misleading myself and my son meant far too much to me for me to implicate him and his memory in something that was not the absolute truth.

Judge the evidence I included in the first chapter. If you can see any other explanation for those incidents than true communication from the afterlife, I would love to know what it is.

I have tried my best to look at the difficult issues faced by the scientists who try to prove that the afterlife of a soul exists. I already have had enough proof of this, but I want to know everything my son went through, and everything about his new home.

To do this, I had to find out how the soul can leave the body with the person's complete memory and personality intact. It is not easy to explain non-physical reality. Right now, we don't know where to start, and the options available depend on mediums who can obtain only so much information for us on where we need to look for the next revolution in human thinking and achievement.

I hope my experience with mediums will be of some help, so those who need to hear from their loved ones have the best experience possible in sad times. Nothing can ever make up for the loss of a dear family member or friend, and the grief is always there. I believe that I'm now meant to spread the truth about the afterlife wherever it needs to be heard.

My courageous and loving son, Jordan, has shown me the way, and I will follow. It is not too late – missed opportunities in the past are in the past and that's where they will stay. I have today, and I have a message of ultimate hope freely given to me that I want share with those who suffer. I do not just believe that we will all be together with those we loved and lost.

I know.
Our loved ones live. Keep the faith.
It will all work out. We are all God.

And nothing can destroy us.

This has been the ultimate gift from my beloved and loving son, Jordan George Jawahir, and in my deep grief, something to cherish.

In loving tribute to my son, Jordan, and with the utmost gratitude, I dedicate this effort to him.

May he never be forgotten
Our love for him will always endure.
Forever.

Dr. George Jawahir, MD
Guelph, Ontario, 2017

Dr. George Jawahir got his BSc. in physiology from the University of Toronto and his medical degree from McMaster in 1984. He joined the Canadian Armed Forces when he started medical school and served until 1990 as a medical officer. George has spent the greater part of his civilian practice in Guelph but quit the practice on the day Jordan died. He has an interest in sports and has multiple permanent injuries to prove it. George lives with his daughter Alannah in Guelph.

CPSIA information can be obtained
at www.ICGtesting.com
Printed in the USA
LVHW11s0855270918
591495LV00005B/9/P